FENG S

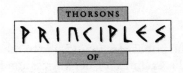

FENG SHUI

SIMON BROWN

Thorsons
An Imprint of HarperCollinsPublishers

The publishers would like to thank
Jillie Collings for her suggestion for
the title of this series, *Principles of...*

Thorsons
An Imprint of HarperCollins*Publishers*
77–85 Fulham Palace Road
Hammersmith, London W6 8JB
1160 Battery Street
San Francisco, California 94111–1213

Published by Thorsons 1996
1 3 5 7 9 10 8 6 4 2

© Simon Brown 1996

Simon Brown asserts the moral right to
be identified as the author of this work

A catalogue record for this book
is available from the British Library

ISBN 0 7225 3347 0

Text illustrations by Jennie Dooge

Printed in Great Britain by
Caledonian Book Manufacturing Ltd, Glasgow

All rights reserved. No part of this publication may be
reproduced, stored in a retrieval system, or transmitted,
in any form or by any means, electronic, mechanical,
photocopying, recording or otherwise, without the prior
permission of the publishers.

CONTENTS

ACKNOWLEDGEMENTS

I would like to start when I began and thank my Mother and Father for giving me so much of their love, enthusiasm and care throughout my life. Dragana for all her passionate love, for bringing me down to earth when I needed it and then picking me up again. I also thank her for spending so much time cooking the most incredible macrobiotic food for me, taking such good care of me and creating a wonderful home for us. Without all this I could not have written this book. My children Christopher, Alexander, Nicholas and Michael, for being so affectionate and so much fun. They have given me the chance to relive my childhood with them. My brother-in-law Denny Waxman, who first introduced me to what was, then, a whole new world of eastern wisdom, for all his help throughout the years, his excellent lectures and most valued friendship. My sister Melanie who introduced me to macrobiotics, invited me to the USA where I met such inspiring teachers, and for taking such good care of me. I wish to thank the rest of my growing family, Adam, Angela, and all my nieces and nephews for giving me so much joy.

Over the years I have met so many teachers who have helped me along this path, and I thank them all. In particular I wish to thank Michio Kushi for inspiring me to make so many positive changes in my life, and all his profound teachings on oriental philosophy and medicine. Shizuko Yamamoto for training me so well in the art of shiatsu, and keeping me focused on real life practical matters. Patrick McCarty, Rik Vermuyten, Patrick Riley and Saul Goodman for being such good teachers in class and so much fun out of class. I have always benefited from and enjoyed my time spent with Marc Van Cauwenberghe, Bill Tara and William Spear.

The aspect of my work I find most enjoyable is the people I meet. Over the years so many of my clients have become good friends. I wish I had the space to mention them all. I would like to give my special thanks to Boy George, Michael Maloney and Kim Andreolli for making my work so exciting and being such good friends. In the same way I have greatly appreciated the company of Bruce Stonehouse, and I would like to thank him for reading the drafts of this book.

I also wish to thank Gina Lazenby and Heidi Gough for their much appreciated work in organizing lectures and clients for me through the Feng Shui Network International. Harriet McNeer who has supported me so much during my visits to the USA, along with Krista and Reid Berman.

I wish to thank all my clients for giving me the benefit of their experience.

Michelle Pilley, from HarperCollins, who commissioned this book, deserves my warmest gratitude for believing in me and in Feng Shui.

Thank you all.

INTRODUCTION

The first time I had the opportunity to put the principles of Feng Shui into practice in a big way was when I bought an apartment in Primrose Hill, London, towards the end of the 1980s. I had already made sure that the direction of my move was favourable to me at that particular time. The apartment, however, needed considerable attention. Not only that but in terms of Feng Shui principles the bathroom was in the ideal location for the kitchen.

We renovated the whole apartment, building new kitchen, dining room and bathroom using as many of the Feng Shui ideas as possible. The end result was a home that was not only a joy to be in, but also a place that I lived in during a very happy phase in my life.

These are my subjective feelings, however they were confirmed when we came to sell the apartment in 1993. Having bought our home at the peak of the property market in London we were now trying to sell at the bottom of the market. People all over the country were experiencing huge losses on their homes. Repossessions by the banks were running high. Neighbours above our apartment had bought theirs at the same time and were also trying to sell. Their home had lost twenty per cent of its value, which was typical across the country. Amazingly three people expressed an interest in our apartment and were willing to pay fifteen per cent more than we had paid in the 1980s. This more than covered the expense of renovation and left us with a reasonable profit.

I followed the same process when moving to my current address. First I found the best directions available to me in that particular year, and then looked at numerous apartments in that favourable direction until I found one that I considered to have the best Feng Shui. One of the reasons for moving was that I had decided to have my office in my home. Since moving this has been very successful for me. My home is constantly receiving visitors and even people who come for the first time are surprised by the bright, sunny atmosphere.

My own definition of Feng Shui is the art of building design that is solely focused on the success of the occupants. Whenever I am involved in a building project or advise someone on improving their home, my main consideration is how I can help them realize their dreams and desires in their lives. My recommendations are designed so that, whenever they are at home, their environment is actually helping their prospects for the future. I apply the same investigation to their place of work. I focus on how to improve the layout of their workplace so that they can be more successful and have happy relationships with their colleagues.

There are many theories on when and how Feng Shui began. One of them is that the ancient civilizations grew along the banks of the River Lo in China. This area was plagued with destructive floods, which ruined the agriculture and buildings. Eventually, around the year 4000 BC, a man named Fu Hsi made many improvements to the river banks that prevented further flooding. He became emperor and the area began to prosper. The area that enjoyed the greatest success was located with the river to the east and protected from the north-east winds. Feng Shui literally translates to Wind Water.

One day, whilst meditating on the banks of the River Lo, Fu Hsi saw a turtle climb out of the water in front of him. Being a symbol of life-long happiness, the turtle has great spiritual significance. However, he was amazed to notice a pattern of black and white dots on the turtle's shell. These dots were arranged in groups from 1 to 9. Not only that, but they were laid out in such a way that whenever they were added together, whether vertically, horizontally or diagonally, they always added up to 15 (see figure 1). Today, this is known as the magic square, and is fundamental to many forms of Feng Shui.

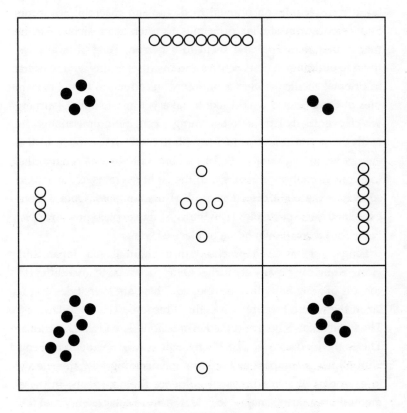

Fig 1 Pattern of black and white dots on the
turtle's shell – The Magic Square

My aim with this book is to explain the essential principles of Feng Shui, and then to show you how to apply them in real life. I began by studying Chinese medicine and philosophy. As time went by I concentrated more on shiatsu, which is a form of acupuncture using hands, rather than needles, to stimulate or relax acupressure points. This proved to be an excellent foundation to my studies as I could later use the ability I developed to feel the movement of energy in a person, to detect the flow of energy in a home. During the course of my studies I first heard about Feng Shui from lectures on oriental medicine and macrobiotics. Feng Shui is based on similar principles to oriental medicine, except that, rather than applying them to a person, Feng Shui applies them to buildings. These lectures and my discussions with masters in oriental medicine were a profound introduction to the principles of Feng Shui. I would like to take you on a similar journey, which eventually led me to becoming a Feng Shui practitioner. To really help you understand Feng Shui I will first explain a) the energy we are working with, b) the forces of yin and yang, c) the five transformations of energy, d) the eight trigrams, e) the magic square, f) the eight directions and g) the compass. Once I have explained these principles I can then go on to explain how to apply Feng Shui to your own home or place of work.

Feng Shui has been practised throughout China, Japan and Hong Kong over many centuries. Over such a large area different schools of Feng Shui have developed. There are four styles popular in the west. They are The Eight Directions, The Eight Houses, The Flying Star School and the Form School. The Eight Directions, The Eight Houses and The Flying Star School methods of Feng Shui all use a compass as the basis for deciding how the energy in each part of a building will influence the occupants. In these methods, the earth's magnetic field, the Sun's solar energy, and the influence of the planets are all thought to have the greatest effect on the way energy flows through a building. These styles of Feng

Shui are closely linked to an oriental form of astrology called Nine Ki astrology.

THE EIGHT DIRECTIONS, OR THE COMPASS METHOD

This method uses a compass to determine the location of eight different areas, each area experiencing a particular type of energy. The features of the house such as the doors, windows and stairs, the function of the rooms such as the kitchen, or the shape of the house, are examined to determine their influence on the home according to the direction in which they lie. In addition, Feng Shui astrology, called Nine Ki, is used to understand and determine the influence of the date and direction of the occupant's move to this building, as well as to establish the ideal time to implement any changes to the building, or to decide when the occupants might initiate important changes in their lives. In addition, the occupants' own Nine Ki chart will influence the recommendations made for their home.

THE EIGHT HOUSE METHOD

This system combines the position of the front of the building with its compass bearing to determine the nature of eight segments, known as houses, within the building. The occupant's own birth date and Nine Ki information then determine the suitability of each of the eight houses within the building for the occupants.

THE FLYING STAR METHOD

With this school the position of the front of the building, with its compass bearing, is used to orientate a chart onto which the building's own birth chart is superimposed. The building's chart is determined by the date it was constructed. The features of the building and the surrounding landscape can then be examined, and their effect on the building's birth chart calculated. In addition, at the beginning of each year, the Nine Ki chart of that year can also be superimposed over the building's chart to provide insights into possible problems in that particular coming year.

THE FORM SCHOOL

The major difference with this method is that a compass is not used at all. The idea is that the way people enter a building determines the way the energy flows through a building. For this reason the main entrance of a building is used to orientate a grid of nine squares, known as the Ba Gua, which then provides information on how each area will effect the occupants.

Practitioners of the first three methods may use a sophisticated form of compass, called a Lo Pan, which is designed to provide extensive information on the eight areas of the building.

I have used both the Form School and the Eight Directions, or Compass method of Feng Shui. I have found the compass method more satisfying for my own style of Feng Shui. In this book I will concentrate on the compass method, along with a basic introduction to the Nine Ki astrology that goes with it.

During the years I have been working as a Feng Shui practitioner I have been to hundreds of homes, offices and businesses. In each building I have made a floor plan, or used existing drawings, and carefully applied the principles of the compass style of Feng Shui. In each case I have listened to the history of what happened to my clients since they moved into this building. By repeatedly going through the same process with each person I have been able to establish in my own mind, how the timing and direction of a move to a new building, along with the building itself, affected the lives of the occupants. I have found that the more experience I gain with examining the history of a building and its occupants, the better I become at being able to advise people on when to move, which directions would be most favourable, and which building would most help them succeed in life.

No building is perfect and most people think there are areas in their life they would like to improve. Therefore a lot of my work involves going to existing buildings and advising the occupants on how to improve their living or working space. With each person I keep my own copy of the drawings, and my written report. This helps me keep in contact over the years and assess the effects of my recommendations.

People often ask me, 'Does Feng Shui really work? What can I expect?' In my opinion Feng Shui is just one piece of the jigsaw puzzle. It is not the jigsaw puzzle itself. I have clients who have experienced amazing results almost immediately. For other clients it has been one small stepping stone on the path to a better quality of life.

When I consider all the different people, their lives and the effects Feng Shui has had, it would be hard to simply answer the above questions. What I have learnt is that a lot depends on what astrological phase the person is in, the direction and timing of their moves, and the way chi energy moves through the building they are in. If only one of these factors is not in someone's favour and it is possible to correct this, then the person can expect much quicker results. For example, someone moves in a good direction to a home, and is in an astrological phase that is supportive to what they want to achieve, but there is a problem with their home. Their bed is in a room where the energy is working against them and the bed itself faces a direction that influences their energy in a way that makes it more difficult for them to succeed in life. Assuming the rest of their home is favourable, by moving their bed to a location that is helping them, they could expect to experience dramatic improvements in the quality of their life.

Much of my work is rather like that of a detective. To work out the best solution to help someone, I first need to find the cause of the problem. This involves a detailed investigation into a) each person's Nine Ki astrological chart, b) their moves, c) the timing of important events in their life, and d) the building they live and/or, work in. Once that is complete I am in a much better position to answer the questions of whether Feng Shui can work for them and to what extent. At that stage I feel more confident about telling people what I feel they can expect and when.

In my opinion Feng Shui does eventually work for everyone. However, the real question is whether a person's expectations of Feng Shui are realistic considering their own situation.

In writing this book I have taken the aspects of Feng Shui that I have found to be most important in my own Feng Shui consultations and concentrated on explaining these as clearly as I can. This book is not intended to be a comprehensive guide to all aspects of Feng Shui. There are many excellent books on Feng Shui available, and I would certainly recommend reading about the various approaches.

I have laid out this book in a similar way to my own Feng Shui consultations. First I will explain the principles of Feng Shui, then how to carry out your own Feng Shui detective work and finally I will describe typical Feng Shui solutions.

PRINCIPLES OF FENG SHUI

CHI ENERGY

Oriental medicine and philosophy is based on the premise that along with all the physical aspects of our world that we can see, hear, touch, smell and taste, there is a movement of a subtle flow of electromagnetic energy. In China this energy is called Chi, in Japan Ki, and in India Prana. Ki is sometimes also spelt Qi.

This Chi energy flows through our bodies in much the same way as our blood. Along the centre of our body are seven large concentrations of Chi energy called Chakras (see Figure 2). Spreading out from the chakras are 14 large paths of Chi energy known as meridians. Twelve of these form pairs and flow along each arm and leg. Like large blood vessels, they take Chi energy to smaller and smaller channels until each cell is nourished by both blood and Chi energy (see Figure 3).

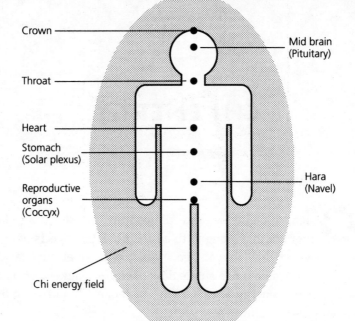

Crown ———

Mid brain
(Pituitary)

Throat ———

Heart ———

Stomach
(Solar plexus)

Hara
(Navel)

Reproductive
organs
(Coccyx)

Chi energy field

Fig 2 Seven large concentrations of energy called Chakras. Chi energy extends typically 10 centimetres to 1 metre outside your skin

Whereas your blood is carrying oxygen and nutrients, such as proteins, carbohydrates, fats, vitamins and minerals, this Chi energy carries your thoughts, ideas, emotions and dreams in life. You may have had the experience of suddenly having a brilliant idea and immediately feeling physically different all over. Many people describe this as a tingling sensation. I believe the flow of Chi energy explains why we feel so different physically, depending on our emotional state. The widespread interest in positive thinking provides one way of learning how to influence the quality of Chi energy flowing through our bodies. If you can train yourself to think about your best character-istics, to plan optimistically for the future and generate feelings

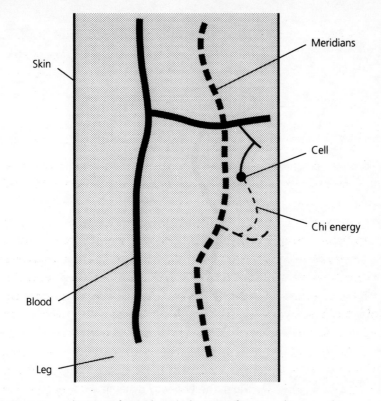

Fig 3 Spreading out from the Chakras are fourteen large paths
of Chi energy known as Meridians.

of love, then it is this kind of energy that will be nourishing all
the cells in your physical body. This could explain why some
people have recovered from life-threatening illnesses by changing the way they think.

One very important aspect is to realize not only that your
thoughts and emotions affect the quality of your Chi energy,
and the Chi energy influences the quality of each of your cells,
but also that the quality of your cells influences the nature of the
Chi energy flowing through them, and this in turn influences
your thoughts. There is a two-way dynamic (see Figure 4).

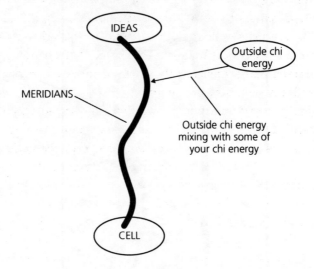

Fig 4 The two-way dynamic

When people come to me for shiatsu, it is usually to treat a physical problem. Yet they are often surprised at how different they feel emotionally after a shiatsu. If during their treatment the flow of their Chi energy has improved it is natural that this will improve their perception of their current emotional state too. In the end they feel better both emotionally and physically.

You may have noticed that if you are feeling depressed, then stimulating physical exercise helps change your mood. Similarly, long slow stretches and deep breathing quickly change your mood if you are angry or tense.

The big difference between Chi energy and your blood is that, apart from menstruation, ideally your blood stays inside your skin, whereas Chi energy extends typically 10 centimetres to 1 metre outside your skin (see Figure 2). This makes your own Chi energy easy to influence. The surrounding Chi energy mixes with some of your Chi energy. I notice a big difference between wearing synthetic clothing and clothes made of natural materials, like cotton, linen or silk. The synthetic fabrics carry a small static charge of electricity which in my experience interferes with my own flow of energy.

Similarly, every building has its own unique movement of Chi energy. I think of this as the atmosphere of a place. In certain buildings one naturally feels more inspired, energetic and more positive. An uplifting atmosphere. However, the reverse is also true. I find spending a few hours in a large building, such as a modern shopping mall or a hospital, is physically draining and mentally disorientating, whereas when I am out in the country, I can walk most of the day and still feel invigorated and emotionally content. In fact I actually end up feeling better. Wherever you are, your own flow of Chi energy is constantly being influenced by your surroundings. Modern buildings often use synthetic carpets, synthetic building materials, artificial lighting and air conditioning.

Not only your clothes and the kind of buildings you are in affect your Chi energy, but also other people's Chi energy, the Chi energy of the surrounding land, and the type of Chi energy created by the weather; all influence your own Chi energy.

Returning to my original definition of Feng Shui, what we are primarily concerned with is what we can do in a building that will help the occupant's own Chi energy flow in a way that will bring on better physical and emotional health. Once we have achieved this, all kinds of possibilities can open up for them. I once described Feng Shui to an acupuncturist friend, as arranging your home so that you are constantly receiving the benefits of an acupuncture treatment. For example, once you

6   have found the ideal location for your bed, those six to eight
hours you lie there will actually be enhancing the flow of Chi
around your body, so that each morning you could awake feeling physically refreshed, emotionally excited about a new day
and clear headed.

On a much broader perspective Chi energy flows not only
throughout our planet, but through the solar system and
galaxy. Our own planet generates a large movement of Chi
energy which flows out and away from the planet, called
Earth's force. At the same time the surrounding planets radiate
energy which travels towards and into the Earth. This energy is
known as Heaven's force (see figure 5). Therefore, the Earth
and surrounding planets have the ability to influence the
movement of Chi energy, which in turn influences our own
individual movement of Chi energy. As the position of the
Earth, Sun and planets changes, so does the way in which Chi
energy moves. Nine Ki astrology is the art of understanding
these large-scale movements of Chi energy and predicting their
effect on a particular person's energy.

Whilst Feng Shui is the understanding of how energy moves
within a certain space, Nine Ki astrology is the study of how
the flow of energy is affected by time. Combined, they provide
a complete consideration of both time and space. For this reason, I also carefully consider the Nine Ki astrological implica-
tions in my reports. For example, the Orange mobile telephone
company employed a Feng Shui consultant not only to help
design their offices, but also to advise on the date to begin their
UK operation.

Perhaps the best way to illustrate the movement of Chi energy would be to imagine zooming away from our planet until
you can look down at the Earth. Pretend you can see the air and
water moving. Some areas will be calm, some will be experiencing quick, almost violent, movements. Chi energy moves in

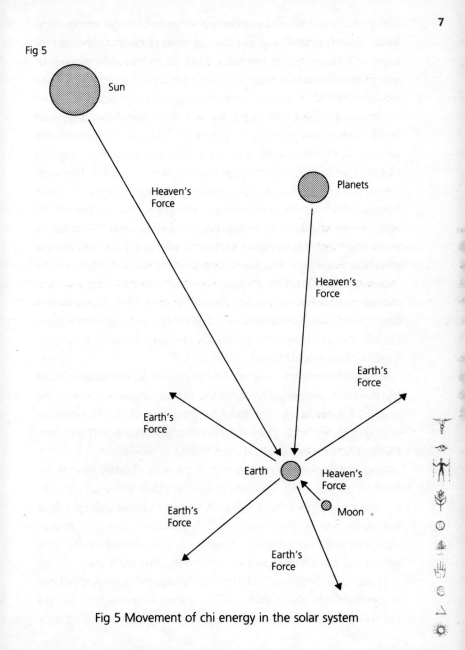

Fig 5 Movement of chi energy in the solar system

similar patterns. One reason why the name Feng Shui, meaning Wind Water, is such a good description, is because the movement of Chi energy mirrors the kind of movements we see in our own wind and water.

For example, visualize fast flowing water passing a sharp point (see Figure 6). As it passes the point, the water begins to swirl, sometimes forming whirlpools. This also happens to air when wind passes a sharp corner. The flow of Chi energy is exactly the same. It swirls around as it passes a protruding corner in a room. This swirling energy is called Cutting Chi and occurs wherever you encounter a sharp protruding corner. In restaurants and hotel lobbies, I have noticed that if a chair is positioned in front of a protruding corner, generally people are reluctant to sit in it. Placing yourself within this swirling spiral of energy will tend to make your own energy swirl around, causing you to feel more disorientated, and more likely to feel confused. Over a long time, such as sleeping in front of such a corner, the constant immersion in swirling energy or cutting Chi could eventually lead to ill health.

Apart from protruding corners there are other influences on the flow of Chi energy to consider. Doors, windows, stairs, the shape of a building, the local landscape and the direction a building faces, will all in their own way influence the movement of Chi energy around your home or office.

Part of a Feng Shui practitioner's job is to identify how these features are affecting the flow of Chi and then find ways to create a more harmonious flow of Chi energy. Often, some areas of the home will be experiencing fast, turbulent energy, whereas others may be very still and stagnant. I aim to create a situation where there is a harmonious flow throughout the home.

When I began Feng Shui, I was fascinated to observe how restaurants and shops in locations with poor Feng Shui would fail. When I talked to people working in one such building they

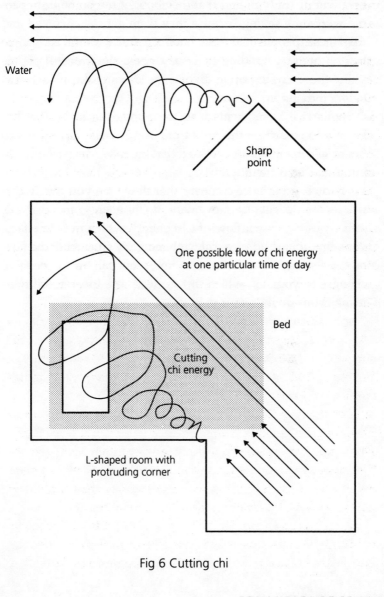

Water

Sharp
point

One possible flow of chi energy
at one particular time of day

Bed

Cutting
chi energy

L-shaped room with
protruding corner

Fig 6 Cutting chi

PRINCIPLES OF FENG SHUI

described it as though the building itself had bad luck. I have had clients who asked me to help because their marriage was breaking up, only to find that they bought the home from people who were selling because they were getting divorced and that these people had also bought from a divorced couple before them. A building that has three generations of people living there, ending up in divorce, needs careful consideration before moving in.

Similarly, I have clients who have bought a home that has been repossessed by the bank from owners who have run into financial difficulties, only to find that they themselves have run into financial difficulties.

My own experience confirms that the home you live in carries its own particular movement of Chi energy, and that this influences your own flow of Chi energy, which in turn effects your emotional and physical well-being. By enhancing the flow of Chi energy in your own home, you can make positive changes to yourself, which in turn lead to a greater ability to realize your own dreams in life.

YIN AND YANG

Chinese Medicine and philosophy, the origins of Feng Shui, are based on the principles of yin and yang. These two words are used to describe everything around us and how this effects us. I assume that when these principles were being developed, people were mainly interested in farming, their basic material needs and health. Yin and yang created a system whereby they could observe what happened in the past and then use this to predict the future.

Let me give you an example. At the time of a full moon, the Chinese would say we become more yang. This means we are more active, want to go out and generally are more social. Now, centuries later, this can be confirmed by statistics; insurance companies will confirm that at the time of a full moon accidents increase, the crime rate in New York goes up and admissions to casualty wards increase. Conversely, at the time of a new moon the ancient Chinese would say that we become more yin, that is more peaceful, more spiritual and more relaxed.

So, armed with this simple piece of yin and yang information, if we wanted to organize a really wild party when would be the best time? The full moon of course. At this time people will be more likely to want to go out and have fun.

The whole point of all this is to be able to do more with your lives with less effort. After all, each of us only has so many years left on this planet, so why not make the most of them. Imagine yourself at the age of ninety. One day you come to the point where you know you are dying and yet you feel very peaceful, relaxed and content. As you look back over the years, you know you lived your life to the full. You can't help but think what a wonderful life you have had. Yin and yang are the tools to help you achieve that. Why be the sort of person who holds a party on a new moon, puts a lot of time and effort into it, only to find that half the people turn up and even then all they want to do is sit around and talk about themselves. The poor hosts get depressed because they think they can't organize a decent party, yet all it was, was bad timing.

The same approach can be applied to food, exercise and our homes. Every home will have areas that will actually help you achieve your aims. Whether you wish to relax, be more inspired, or have increased energy, the secret is to find the place that has the atmosphere and environment to support you.

Yin and yang are the first of the essential points to be grasped in understanding the frameworks used in Feng Shui. To communicate and learn from experience, we need some kind of framework. For example, simple maths, like addition, provides us with the framework to do everyday activities such as shopping. We use it for counting the number of groceries we need, adding up the cost, or adding the weights of ingredients. In this context it works and we use it every day to our mutual benefit.

However, adding numbers together only works some of the time in real life and is often only an approximation. For example, if we take two drops of water and add them to another two drops of water, we only have one drop of water instead of four. If we were to weigh the drops of water, we would find that each drop is in the process of changing its weight. It may be evaporating or absorbing dust. In any case, our weighing machine will also be in a process of change, expanding or contracting, depending on variations in temperature. In the end, we can only say that if we take four drops of water, each weighing one gram, and put them all together, we will end up with approximately four grams. Yin and yang is a similar framework. By studying yin and yang, you can learn more about your environment and how it effects you, in a much shorter time than if you were to try solely by your own random experiences. Once you and a friend have a basic understanding of yin and yang, you then have the language to discuss your experiences of your environment to a much deeper level.

The point is, all the ideas in this book are here to help you understand what is going on around and within you, and to then be able to communicate with others. Once you try to think of any of these frameworks as rigid absolutes, they become difficult to understand. Just as trying to explain mathematical addition to someone who is putting drops of water together will seem ridiculous, the same is true of Feng Shui. Fortunately, the principles of Feng Shui have been around for thousands of years, plenty of time for people to try them out, question their validity and develop their practical application.

My advice is to keep an open mind, try to first understand the principles as frameworks and then test them in real life.

The Yellow Emperor's Classic of Internal Medicine tells us that by 2600 BC the Chinese people already had a great interest in the subjective effects of their environment. It describes how they had evolved the concept of a pair of interactive polarities present throughout nature, which they termed yin and yang. Nothing was seen to be absolutely yin or yang, but simply more yin or more yang when compared to something else. For example, resting is a more yin state than working, but more yang when compared to sleeping.

In ancient China it was observed that in the morning, as the sun comes up, people are naturally more active and alert, a more yang characteristic than resting. In contrast, during the afternoon, people generally feel more mentally orientated, physically passive and sometimes even sleepy, which is a more yin characteristic. The classic definition of yin and yang is the shady and sunny side of the mountain, the sunny side being yang. Similarly, the sunny side of your home is considered to be more yang, whereas the northern, shady side is more yin (if you live in the northern hemisphere).

I remember living in a flat near Primrose Hill, London, where the front of the house faced north and the back south. All the bedrooms were on the north side. These rooms had a dark, almost cave-like quality, that I and my family found ideal for sleeping. However, no daytime activity worked there. The children would never play in their bedroom, even though we had arranged it to be a fun playroom. During the day we all wanted to be in the southern, sunny side of the flat.

As you can imagine, when the sun is up, the southern side of a home is constantly being irradiated by the Sun's energy. People in this side of the home will benefit from this Chi energy. So if you want to have more energy, to be active and inspired, place yourself in a part of your home that benefits from the sunlight. This still works on a cloudy day. Apart from heat and light, the sun radiates solar energy and Chi energy. Just like my example with the moon, here you will feel you can do more with less effort. However, during the course of many of my Feng Shui consultations I have found people trying to work in the shady side of a building, and not having the energy to get things done. I remember one client who could hardly stay awake in the afternoons. She would keep drifting off in front of her computer. Once I found a more energetic place for her, she soon noticed the difference. I have also met clients who themselves are of a lively nature, working in a very high energy, sunny part of their building, finding it very difficult to concentrate and focus. For them, a less active place is actually more productive. Each person is different and the art is to find what really works for that individual.

Growing up in England I was fascinated by the different cultures in southern Europe. The people I met in countries like Italy, Yugoslavia, Spain and Greece were so lively and expressive. They talked quickly, gesticulated wildly and seemed very passionate. In the towns, people drove fast and there was often the sound of car horns. When it came to getting on a bus, everyone wanted to pile on at the same time, as soon as the bus arrived. All characteristics of more yang forms of expression than I was used to. When I began to study yin and yang this all began to make more sense. They were living on the sunny side of the mountain, or in this case the sunny side of Europe.

The idea of balance is fundamental to yin and yang thinking. Everything is trying to be in balance. However, to be more balanced, it may require unhealthy extremes of either yin or yang. For example, a long period of severe stress, which is more yang, might be balanced by that person having a nervous breakdown, which is more yin. We try to maintain some kind of balance all the time. If you give guests at a party or customers at a pub, dry, salty snacks, which are more yang type foods, they will tend to crave liquid or sweets which are comparatively yin. The same is true the other way around. Lots of fruits, salads and drinks, which are more yin, will create a craving for salty, savoury foods. We tend to continually swing from yin to yang. Sometimes we become more yang, and we then try to find ways to become more yin. Once we have become more yin we want to feel more yang again, and so it goes on.

This cause and effect also applies to the weather. In the autumn and winter the air becomes more cold and damp, both yin qualities. This creates a need for warming foods like hot porridge, thick soups and stews, which are more yang, creating balance in the body. Conversely, in the spring and summer, as the air becomes warmer and dryer, a more yang atmosphere, people then prefer yin quality foods that will cool the body, such as fruits, salads and drinks. As everything moves in a cycle of constant change yin always changes to yang and back again. This constant flow can be seen throughout our natural environment. The day (yang) changes to night (yin). After we rest (yin) we go to work (yang).

People can also be more yin or yang. A more yin person tends to be relaxed, physically supple, sensitive, creative and imaginative. However, if this person is too yin they could become lethargic, slow and depressed. The opposite is true of someone more yang. A more yang person tends to be alert, quick, more physically active, able to concentrate and pay attention to detail. But if the person becomes too yang they would become tense, irritable, angry or physically stiff and tight. People are a mixture of both yin and yang. With a health problem the overriding cause can frequently be attributed to an extreme of yin or yang.

All this becomes very powerful when you can actually control these natural processes to achieve certain results. For example, with a simple understanding of yin and yang one can tailor one's diet, exercise and lifestyle to one's own individual needs. If you have a very demanding event next week, between now and then, you would benefit from eating more yang foods and doing more yang exercises. After this event, more yin foods and exercises would be ideal to relax and unwind you.

In terms of a house, buildings that have sharp, straight lines, sharp corners and are very angular, are more yang than those that are more rounded, irregular and curved.

You can make your home more yin by adding soft surfaces such as tapestries, big cushions and long curtains. In contrast, tiles, metal surfaces and glass create a more yang atmosphere.

Colours have a great influence. Bright, strong, stimulating colours make us feel more yang, whereas soft, relaxing colours make us more yin. People have their own individual reactions to colours. However, red, orange and bright yellow are examples of colours that make us feel more yang. Greens, blues and pastel shades help us feel more yin.

One of the ways I test the principles of Feng Shui is to observe the most successful restaurants and compare them with those sites that have a high turnover of restaurant failures. The successful restaurants have often applied Feng Shui by chance or by design with great accuracy. A relatively new chain of fast food restaurant opening branches throughout London, predominantly uses shiny stainless steel on their walls, along with a maroon, purple colour. The decoration gives the restaurants a strong yang impression. Purple is considered the colour of passion. This is ideal for being noticed. As you walk by, you can't help but look in. All those bright sparkling surfaces. Once you enter and are inside and seated, you can't wait to get out. It's too yang. Of course, this is just what you want if you are the owner of a fast food restaurant. Lots of customers coming in, buying food and leaving quickly. You will notice that shiny plastic, bright lights, tiles and metal surfaces, are a consistent theme in fast food restaurants. Conversely, we find it hard to imagine sleeping in a room constructed from metal, tiles and glass. History has shown that we like soft yin furnishings in our bedroom.

The easiest way to decide if you are too yin or yang is to compare yourself to other people. I have a friend who consistently finds other people aggressive and pushy. To her, everyone else is too yang. She often wakes late. She daydreams and burns the porridge. Her boyfriend becomes annoyed with her. She rushes for the bus without the correct money. People in the queue become irritable as she fumbles for the change. She is late. Her boss is annoyed. Once at work she wants to relax, chat and socialize. Her colleagues push her to get on and finish things. And so it goes on. Compared to most other people she is more yin. At the same time there must be something very yang present to maintain balance. Perhaps a very yang experience from the past, something in her diet that is too yang or even working in a very yang building/environment could be the cause.

On the other hand, when I worked as an engineer, I had a colleague who found everyone else far too yin. He was constantly complaining that people were too slow. Why couldn't they get on with their lives. He was always rushing, getting furious with anyone who slowed him down. He was great with details, but broad-ranging, imaginative discussions on a point of design would drive him mad. He did a lot of shouting. Everything seemed to be a source of irritation. Working with my more yin colleagues would have sent him into a rage. Compared with other people in the design office he was much more yang. How did he get his balance of yin? As soon as he finished work he would rush round to the pub for a couple of pints of beer before going home.

So, each person has more yin or yang characteristics and our environment has the ability to make us more yin or more yang. The idea is that if you can recognize whether you are already too yin or too yang, you can then decide if you need to become more yin or more yang in order to feel happier and more balanced. Once you know this, you can change your environment in a way that helps you become more yin or more yang.

To illustrate this, let us take the example of a man who finds he becomes irritable and angry at work. He realizes that his conduct is becoming a serious problem in terms of the success of his career. Not only that, but women find him aggressive and intimidating. The first assessment we need to make is whether his behaviour is more yin or yang. My opinion is that we can safely assume he is more yang. If he can become more yin, he will be more relaxed, calmer and have a greater feeling of peace inside himself. How can we change his home to help him become more yin?

Let us take his bedroom for this example. Here are the things I would look for to avoid. Hard shiny surfaces such as mirrors. Furniture with sharp edges. Objects with bright stimulating colours, such as a picture of a bright red racing car. Objects made of hard materials. This could include metal furniture, steel ornaments or wrought iron artifacts. Wall colours that are too stimulating. Steel blinds on his windows. Brightly-coloured bed clothes.

The next step is to advise him what to replace these yang features with. My recommendation would be to bring more of the following into his bedroom. Objects and furniture with more round, curved shapes. Colours that help him relax. Perhaps greens. Cloth wall hangings. Loose curtains. Furniture made of wood rather than metal. Plants with large, round, floppy leaves instead of wrought iron. Calming colours for his bedding.

The philosophy of yin and yang is open to many interpretations and this chapter owes a great debt to the work of the Japanese author George Ohsawa.

THE FIVE ELEMENTS OF CHI ENERGY

To help understand the process I am taking you through, imagine we are building a house. The foundation represents an understanding of Chi energy. The first floor is the philosophy of yin and yang. Now we are ready to add a new floor. This next layer of understanding is the Five Elements of Chi Energy. Also called the Five Transformations of Chi Energy. Essentially, this is a further refinement of yin and yang. Whereas yin and yang express two opposite, but complementary characteristics, the five elements describe five different types of Chi energy.

The five elements are based on the annual seasons. Rather than the four seasons we are used to, this is based on a year divided into five distinct seasons. The additional season appears between what we think of as summer and autumn. It is called early autumn or late summer. I will refer to it as early autumn. Each of the five elements describes a certain kind of Chi energy. To discover the characteristics of each Chi energy, think of the atmosphere at that time of year. In addition, each time of year is associated with a particular element to further describe the quality of that particular energy. In a medical context we can also add pairs of organs and human emotions.

Figure 7 shows each of the five elements, with the appropriate

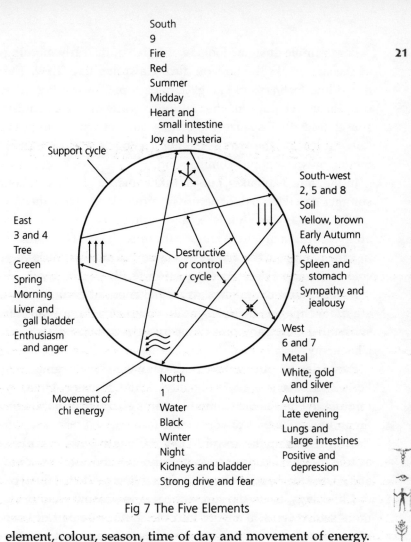

South
9
Fire
Red
Summer
Midday
Heart and
    small intestine
Joy and hysteria

Support cycle

South-west
2, 5 and 8
Soil
Yellow, brown
Early Autumn
Afternoon
Spleen and
    stomach
Sympathy and
    jealousy

East
3 and 4
Tree
Green
Spring
Morning
Liver and
    gall bladder
Enthusiasm
    and anger

Destructive
or control
cycle

West
6 and 7
Metal
White, gold
    and silver
Autumn
Late evening
Lungs and
    large intestines
Positive and
    depression

Movement of
chi energy

North
1
Water
Black
Winter
Night
Kidneys and bladder
Strong drive and fear

Fig 7 The Five Elements

element, colour, season, time of day and movement of energy. The numbers refer to the Nine Ki numbers of the magic square. This will be explained later in the book. The idea is that you develop an understanding of the nature of the Chi energy at each phase based on real life experiences. (I have also added the organs and emotions, although this aspect of the five elements will not be covered further.)

22   For example, imagine looking at a tree in the early morning as the sun breaks the horizon during a spring day (Tree). The overriding feeling is of energy moving up. Contrast this with the early evening in the autumn watching a beautiful sunset (Metal). Visualize the setting sun reflecting off metal railway tracks The overwhelming feeling is of Chi energy moving inwards and becoming solid.

In the same way take yourself to the middle of a bright, hot, summer day (Fire). All of nature is in full bloom. Now the Chi energy feels as though it is expanding in every direction, radiating heat like a fire. Next jump to the opposite (Water). A freezing, foggy night in the middle of winter. The atmosphere is very cold and damp. Everything is quiet and still.

Finally, think of walking across fields on an early autumn afternoon. Imagine the soil beneath your feet. Heavy, solid and substantial. These are some of the qualities associated with soil Chi energy.

Every day the sun will move through the sky, charging your home with solar energy. The quality of this Chi energy will vary through the day as the sun moves through different phases. In the morning the part of your home facing east, where the sun rises, will soak up the upward kind of Chi energy we described as tree. As the day progresses, the sun will move to the south and charge up the southern part of your home with the fire type of Chi energy. Later, the sun will begin to go down and bring more settled soil Chi energy into the south-west part of your home. As the sun sets in the west, the western part of your home will take in metal Chi energy. Finally, during the night, the north of your home benefits from water Chi energy. Soil Chi energy is assocaited with the centre of your home.

Each of the five elements has a colour that most closely represents the nature of the particular Chi energy.

Green is the colour that is considered to most closely represent the tree Chi energy found in the east. This is considered to represent life, growth and vitality. The shade of green needs to make you feel uplifted, refreshed and alive to have its desired effect.

Red is the colour that represents the fire Chi energy of the south. The midday sun, summer and heat can all be found in this colour. The shade of red would ideally instil feelings of passion, excitement and warmth.

Yellow and brown are the colours that are considered closest to the soil Chi energy of the south west and centre. Autumn in the northern hemisphere is coloured with brown leaves. Both yellow and brown can create a more settled, comfortable atmosphere. The shades of these colours should be chosen for their ability to bring out feelings of security.

White, gold and silver represent the Chi energy of the element of metal. These colours of the west are selected to create a solid, rich atmosphere.

Black is the colour that is closest to the water Chi energy found in the north. Ideally, the use of black will bring out and accentuate feelings of depth, power and flexibility.

Later in the book I will explain how nine different kinds of Chi energy can be used in Feng Shui. In this system the allocation of colours is different.

Think about your home and how each room is affected by the movement of the Sun. This will begin to help you decide which activities are best suited to which parts of your home.

I expect you will find the east is ideal for activities that require more up energy. Planning your day, morning exercises or starting new projects will all work well here.

The south, fire energy, is outgoing and better for parties, social events and having fun.

The more settled energy of the south-west and centre makes

this a better place for practical projects, such as hobbies, DIY projects or arts and crafts.

The west of your home is where you will find the big red sunsets, making this a romantic place to relax and conclude your day.

The north, being winter and night, makes this an obvious place to sleep.

Remember, each home is different, and these suggestions are broad generalizations. Later, we will examine each direction in more detail.

For now, the most important step is to understand the character of each part of the cycle and next, how they relate to each other.

I shall use the yearly agricultural seasons to describe the way each part of the cycle relates to the other elements in the cycle. In this analogy we will plant a seed in winter and watch it grow through each of the five seasons until the plant seeds itself in the late autumn.

In winter we prepare the ground and plant seeds. If the next stage, spring, is favourable, our seeds will begin to sprout and grow. However, if the spring has late frosts, then the crop will be destroyed, with nothing to show in the summer. Basically, the water element supports the tree element, however, if the tree energy is deficient and water energy jumps across to fire, the process becomes destructive. In the same way you could think of water feeding a tree, but putting out a fire.

Assuming a good winter and spring, then during the summer the fields will be full of crops. Now, if the summer is poor, due to lack of sunshine and heavy rains, our crops will start to rot in the ground in the early autumn. Tree Chi energy supports fire, like putting wood on a fire, whereas a lack of fire Chi energy will allow tree Chi energy to destroy soil Chi energy.

If the winter, spring and summer have been good for the crops, they will ripen and become sweet during the early autumn. If the early autumn has frosts or heavy rains, the crops will spoil before they produce seeds or are ready to be harvested in the late autumn. Here fire Chi energy supports early soil Chi energy, but a weak soil Chi energy allows fire Chi energy to destroy metal Chi energy.

If the conditions during winter, spring, summer and early autumn were all good, then there will be a magnificent harvest in the late autumn and seeds to plant in the winter. If this stage is incomplete then we cannot begin the cycle again. This time, soil Chi energy supports metal Chi energy, but when metal Chi energy is weak, soil Chi energy will destroy water Chi energy.

Finally, if the winter is poor the conditions will not be suitable for planting the seeds. Metal Chi energy will override the weak water Chi energy and destroy the tree Chi energy.

In Figure 7, the circle around the outside represents what is often referred to as the support cycle, whereas the lines inside the cycle depict the destructive cycle. The destructive cycle is not necessarily a bad thing and in certain situations can be useful in Feng Shui.

In Feng Shui it is common to use the five elements such as actual water, fire or metal in real life to encourage changes in the movement of Chi energy. For example, it is considered auspicious to have water to the east of your home. This places water in a direction from your home that relates to the tree element. The water Chi energy supports tree Chi energy. Therefore water to the east will enhance the movement of upward energy found in the east.

The support cycle can also be used to calm Chi energy down. This time, let us assume we have found too much Chi energy in the south-west. The south-west is associated with soil Chi energy. Placing something made of metal in this location will have the effect of absorbing some of the soil Chi energy, as soil Chi energy supports metal Chi energy. This could be a metal wind chime, large clock or metal ornament.

The position of a working fireplace requires careful consideration. Placing the fireplace in the south part of your home, also the element of fire, can make the fire Chi energy too strong. Complementary elements would be tree and soil.

The east part of your home, tree Chi energy, is recommended for a kitchen as water and fire, both commonly found in kitchens, are in harmony with tree Chi energy.

Colours can be used in the same way. The colour of fire Chi energy is red. If you want to increase fire Chi energy in the south, then the tree Chi energy colour green will behave as a supporting colour. To calm down fire Chi energy, a soil Chi energy colour, yellow or brown, will take some of the fire Chi energy away. A water Chi energy colour, black, will tend to destroy the fire Chi energy, if the colour green is missing.

To summarize, the five elements describe five different kinds of Chi energy. The easiest way to understand the characteristics of each of these five types of Chi energy is to remember the kind of atmosphere you experience during the season that each type of Chi energy is associated with. In addition, each of the five types of Chi energy has an element that also describes its nature.

Each of the five types of Chi energy has a special relationship with the other four kinds of Chi energy. Look at Figure 7 and start with the fire element. This kind of Chi energy will naturally support the next type of Chi energy (soil) when following the arrows in a clockwise direction. If the next Chi energy (soil) is weak, the one after the weak Chi energy (metal) will be overwhelmed, and destroyed by the Chi energy we started with (fire).

At the same time the element we first picked (fire) is supported by the preceding type of Chi energy (tree). However, if the tree Chi energy is weak, then the type of Chi energy before that (water) will destroy the kind of Chi energy we started with (fire).

THE MAGIC SQUARE

As described in the introduction, Fu Hsi first discovered the Magic Square when a turtle climbed out of the River Lo, around 4000 BC in China. The pattern of dots on its shell led Fu Hsi to discover the pattern of numbers that has become the basis of Nine Ki astrology, and many styles of Feng Shui.

Thinking of the imaginary house, we are now adding another floor. On this third floor the idea is to examine nine different ways in which Chi energy can move. So we have gone from looking at Chi energy as a whole, to two types of Chi energy, yin and yang, to five kinds of Chi energy known as the Five Elements of Energy, and now nine different Chi energy types.

Figure 8 shows all nine types of Nine Ki charts. The chart in the middle is called the Standard Chart. This is the chart where the numbers always add up to 15, whether you add them vertically, horizontally or diagonally. This standard chart always has the number 5 in its centre.

Surrounding the standard chart, I have drawn eight different charts with the numbers 1, 2, 3, 4, 6, 7, 8 and 9 in the centre. Each chart is referred to by its central number. So the standard chart is called the chart of five. The chart with 9 in the middle will be called the chart of nine and so on. Every year, month,

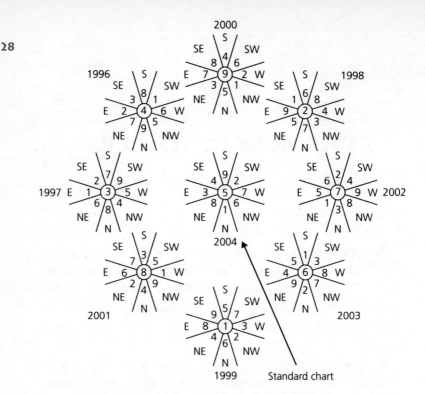

Fig 8 Nine Ki charts with examples of the chart
for each year until 2004

day and hour is represented by one of these charts. For the pur-
pose of the Feng Shui studies I will concentrate solely on the
years.

Each year has its own Nine Ki number that takes up the central position in the chart for that particular year. The number of
the year decreases by 1 as a new Nine Ki year begins. The number in the centre of the chart for 1996 is 4. We can say 1996 is a
4 year. 1997 is a 3 year, 1998 a 2 year and so on.

From this you can work out which number was in the centre
of the chart in the year you were born. This is called your Nine
Ki Year number.

Your Nine Ki Year Number	9	8	7	6	5	4	3	2	1
Year	1901	1902	1903	1904	1905	1906	1907	1908	1909
Date	4 Feb	5 Feb	5 Feb	5 Feb	4 Feb	4 Feb	5 Feb	5 Feb	4 Feb
Time	19:03	00:57	06:55	12:40	18:36	00:28	06:13	12:09	17:53
	1910	1911	1912	1913	1914	1915	1916	1917	1918
	4 Feb	5 Feb	5 Feb	4 Feb	4 Feb	5 Feb	5 Feb	4 Feb	4 Feb
	23:41	05:33	11:11	17:01	22:53	04:34	10:31	16:18	22:06
	1919	1920	1921	1922	1923	1924	1925	1926	1927
	5 Feb	5 Feb	4 Feb	4 Feb	5 Feb	5 Feb	4 Feb	4 Feb	5 Feb
	04:00	09:43	15:34	21:28	03:13	09:06	14:58	20:49	02:46
	1928	1929	1930	1931	1932	1933	1934	1935	1936
	5 Feb	4 Feb	4 Feb	5 Feb	5 Feb	4 Feb	4 Feb	5 Feb	5 Feb
	08:31	14:19	20:11	01:53	07:42	13:28	19:13	01:03	06:47
	1937	1938	1939	1940	1941	1942	1943	1944	1945
	4 Feb	4 Feb	5 Feb	5 Feb	4 Feb	4 Feb	4 Feb	5 Feb	4 Feb
	12:36	18:32	00:20	06:15	12:07	17:57	23:51	05:39	11:26
	1946	1947	1948	1949	1950	1951	1952	1953	1954
	4 Feb	4 Feb	5 Feb	4 Feb	4 Feb	4 Feb	5 Feb	4 Feb	4 Feb
	17:18	23:03	04:50	10:40	16:29	22:29	04:07	09:52	15:42
	1955	1956	1957	1958	1959	1960	1961	1962	1963
	4 Feb	5 Feb	4 Feb	4 Feb	4 Feb	5 Feb	4 Feb	4 Feb	4 Feb
	21:29	03:15	09:07	14:57	20:47	02:38	08:29	14:24	20:17
	1964	1965	1966	1967	1968	1969	1970	1971	1972
	5 Feb	4 Feb	4 Feb	4 Feb	5 Feb	4 Feb	4 Feb	4 Feb	5 Feb
	02:28	07:57	13:46	19:32	01:19	07:04	12:50	18:37	00:23
	1973	1974	1975	1976	1977	1978	1979	1980	1981
	4 Feb	4 Feb	4 Feb	4 Feb	4 Feb	4 Feb	4 Feb	4 Feb	4 Feb
	06:13	12:08	17:56	23:48	05:38	11:28	17:21	23:10	04:59
	1982	1983	1984	1985	1986	1987	1988	1989	1990
	4 Feb	4 Feb	4 Feb	4 Feb	4 Feb	4 Feb	4 Feb	4 Feb	4 Feb
	10:53	16:38	22:27	04:18	10:05	15:57	21:42	05:28	09:20
	1991	1992	1993	1994	1995	1996	1997	1998	1999
	4 Feb	4 Feb	4 Feb	4 Feb	4 Feb	4 Feb	4 Feb	4 Feb	4 Feb
	15:04	20:51	02:42	08:27	14:18	20:10	02:00	08:01	13:51
	2000	2001	2002	2003	2004	2005	2006	2007	2008
	4 Feb	4 Feb	4 Feb	4 Feb	4 Feb	4 Feb	4 Feb	4 Feb	4 Feb
	19:39	01:35	07:20	13:08	18:57	00:38	06:31	12:16	17:59
	2009	2010	2011	2012	2013	2014	2015	2016	2017
	3 Feb	4 Feb	4 Feb	4 Feb	3 Feb	4 Feb	4 Feb	4 Feb	3 Feb
	23:55	05:40	11:31	17:28	23:05	05:05	10:55	16:40	22:37

The year you were born with the date and time the year begins.
The times the year changes are in Greenwich Mean Time (GMT)

Fig 9 The Nine Ki Year numbers with the starting date and time for the years 1901 to 2017

Figure 9 shows the Nine Ki Year number for each of the years in this century. It is important to note that the Nine Ki year does not start on 1 January, as it does in the western calendar. Usually it is 3, 4 or 5 February. I have included the exact date and time each year begins in the table. So a person born in the month of January or the first few days of February will actually base their Nine Ki Year number on the preceding year. For example, if you were born on 1 February 1962, you would actually use the chart for 1961. The same applies when moving. If you move home on 1 February 1997, you actually use the chart for 1996. We will go into more detail about moving in chapter 9.

The times are given in Greenwich Mean Time (GMT). If you are born close to the time at which the year changes you may need to convert the time to your local time. For example, the year changes at 09:07 on 4 February 1957. To convert to New York time, subtract five hours. So in New York the year changes at 04:07 on 4 February.

The idea is that in the year of each person's birth, the Earth, Sun, Moon and surrounding planets exerted their combined influence in such a way that it left an imprint on each person 's Chi energy. In the same way that each one of us has a distinct and unique thumbprint, our Chi energy tends to flow in a specific pattern.

Once you understand the way your own Chi energy moves, it is then possible to predict how it will mix with the predominant Chi energy of any year. For example, someone who was born after 14:24 (GMT) on 3 February 1962, was born in a year when 2 was in the centre of the chart. Therefore, their Nine Ki Year number is 2. After 20:10 (GMT) on 3 February 1996 the number at the centre for that year is 4. By analyzing how someone with the Chi energy represented by the Nine Ki Year number 2 mixes with the Chi energy present in a Nine Ki Year when 4 is in the middle, it is possible to predict how they will fare that year. Most importantly this will provide essential information to advise them on how they can make the most of that year.

In this example someone with the Nine Ki Year number 2 will be in the east position in 1996. For them 1996 would be an excellent year to start a new business, begin a career or gain promotion. I would expect 1996 to be a busy active year for someone with the Nine Ki Year number 2. This will be explained in more detail in chapter 9.

In addition, every year each person's own Chi energy will mix best with Chi energies found in one or more of the eight directions. Therefore, by moving to a new home or office in a certain direction at a specific time, you can actually enhance your own Chi energy. Unfortunately, moving to a Chi energy that does not support your own Chi energy can harm the movement of your own Chi. In my experience people often find that when they move home, profound changes in their lives follow. By carefully examining a person's own chart and the chart for the year in which they wish to move, it is possible to predict the kind of changes they could expect.

Firstly, it is important to remember that the central number decreases by 1 as each year passes and that the eight numbers around the central number move into a new pattern each year. Second, you must be able to find your Nine Ki Year number, which is the number that was in the centre of the chart during the year you were born.

To calculate the Nine Ki Year number for a woman an alternative system uses the reverse process where, instead of each year decreasing by 1, it increases by 1. The numbers for both male and female are the same when their Nine Ki Year number is 3. However, keeping to the system I have the most experience with I will continue with the method where the same Nine Ki Year number is used for females and males.

THE EIGHT DIRECTIONS

I n this chapter I will examine each of the nine numbers and build every one into a character that describes the kind of movement of Chi energy it represents. In this context the numbers themselves are not important. They are simply the names given to nine different types of Chi energy.

Think back to my analogy of building a house. A point of possible confusion is that each of the floors or layers of understanding does not necessarily match the others. To some people this is a source of frustration. However, as a practitioner I find it provides a greater ability to find a solution for each unique situation. Applying yin and yang to someone's home will lead to certain recommendations, whereas the Five Transformations of Chi energy can provide the insights to find alternative suggestions. In the same way the eight directions may orientate the study of a person's home in such a way that it leads to still different conclusions. Using a combination of all of them is most powerful.

In chapter 2 I mentioned how careful one must be when applying simple maths to real life. The same is true of Feng Shui. However, in this approach to Feng Shui there are different layers to apply to different situations. An experienced practitioner will have learnt that sometimes one particular layer may have greater use than other layers.

TRIGRAM	DIRECTION	SYMBOL	FIVE ELEMENT	NINE KI	FAMILY MEMBER
	North	Water	Water	1	Middle son
	North-east	Mountain	Soil	8	Youngest son
	East	Thunder	Tree	3	Eldest son
	South-east	Wind	Tree	4	Eldest Daughter
	South	Fire	Fire	9	Middle daughter
	South-west	Earth	Soil	2	Mother
	West	Lake	Metal	7	Youngest daughter
	North-west	Heaven	Metal	6	Father

Fig 10 Trigrams. Later Heaven Sequence

Each direction has a trigram associated with it. A trigram is basically three lines (see Figure 10). The lines can either be solid or broken. The solid lines are more yang and the broken lines more yin. These eight trigrams are found in the ancient Chinese text called *The I Ching*. In this book the trigrams are placed in pairs giving a total of six solid or broken lines. These are called hexagrams. There are a total of 64 ways in which the six lines in each hexagram can be arranged as a combination of solid and broken lines. There are eight combinations in which the solid or broken lines of the trigrams can be arranged.

The Nine Ki number 5 does not have a Trigram or direction as it is situated in the centre. For this reason 5 is considered the most powerful of all the numbers.

Each trigram has:

a   a direction that describes the Chi energy in that direction. There are two ways in which the trigrams can be applied to each direction. In this book I use the Later Heaven Sequence.

b   one of the five elements associated with it. In addition, where more than one trigram is associated with one of the five elements, the trigrams have their own symbol.

c   a Nine Ki number and its colour that reflects the nature of the Chi energy and a time of day when the Chi energy in this part of the home is strongest.

d   a member of the family that further describes the Chi energy.

The references to the family are based on a traditional oriental family, whose roles may now seem out of date compared to a modern western society. Referring to the members of the family is intended to help understand the nature of that particular trigram.

To build up a complete picture I will keep adding to the character of each number. One way to do this is to describe each number using the analogy of the cycle of life. I will use the examples of a human being and a plant. By examining the various stages during the cycle of life you can better understand the way Chi energy moves within a building.

At the same time remember your own Nine Ki Year number and see if the description for your number applies to a part of your character. A proper Nine Ki astrology chart consists of much more information than your Nine Ki Year number. The month and day will all play an important part in describing the energy present on the day you were born. However, you may recognize a part of yourself in my description of your relevant Chi energy based solely on the kind of Chi energy present during the year you were born.

Additionally, I have shown the various effects of having the main door in each of the directions from the centre of the building. The gate to the land on which the building sits and the main door into the building are important features in terms of the flow of energy through a building. These influences are described in more detail later in the book.

I have written a description for every colour that is associated with each of the trigrams and the centre position. Apart from the colours of the east and the centre position, soil 5, all of these colours are different from those in the five elements.

Each direction can now be described as follows.

ONE NORTH

Five Element	Water
Symbol	Water
Family Member	Middle son
Colour	Off white
Time	Night

The north part of a home has a quiet energy that is associated with sex, spirituality and isolation. Although this energy is passive on the surface, it carries a great power deeper inside. The image of the middle son is one that is affectionate, but independent from the family. It is an energy that carries a great independent spirit. The north energy also helps the occupants make deep changes within themselves.

In the cycle of life north represents conception. In a human being this is the phase of internal development. In the case of a seed it is when the germ of the seed begins to eat the fruit of the seed inside the husk. This is also an internal process where energy is kept inside. In a human being this energy represents more deep internal processes and thoughts. So far the seed is not dependent on its outside environment so it shows great independence. On the surface all appears very quiet. However, deep inside powerful changes are taking place.

If a building had the main door in this darker, colder position, it could lead to feelings of isolation. It is said that a door in the north is ideal for hiding. I would not recommend a door in the north for anyone who would like an active life. I have several clients who, having moved to a home with the main door in the north, complain that they feel lonely.

The energy in the north of a building is most suited to activities such as sleep, sex, meditation and creative activities that require solitude. Rooms that would suit this kind of energy are a bedroom, meditation room or an artist's studio if the artist likes to develop independently. Within a building the area to the north of the centre will be helpful if you wish to feel more quiet, independent and find an inner peace.

The colour associated with water is off white. This shade of white has an almost translucent quality, most easily produced with a gloss finish. Ideally, it would convey an impression of depth and movement, with flexibility. Water Chi energy can change direction easily, but in a way that does not disturb the surrounding Chi energy too much.

Five Element	Soil
Symbol	Mountain
Family Member	Youngest son
Colour	White
Time	Early morning

The north-east section of a building carries a strong piercing energy. The symbol of the mountain creates a more rocky, harsh atmosphere. The youngest son has the image of a more spoilt, competitive child, who will put so much energy into getting his own way that others tend to give in. The Chi energy here is motivating, sharp and direct. In addition the Chi energy of the north-east is very quick to change direction.

Now in the cycle of life the child has been born and is engaged with learning to interact with his or her environment. The baby has to take in oxygen from the air, and later eat food from nature. The child becomes self-motivated, and as time goes by develops a strong identity of self. Many parents will recognize this as 'the terrible twos' when their child no longer shares his or her toys, and has tantrums when they cannot get their own way. In a seed this is the phase when the young plant begins to grow, sprouting its shoot and root. For the first time the seed starts to take in nourishment from the soil. This is a stage where the seed has to establish itself and its territory. This is a highly self-motivated stage, in which there is a strong element of competition, directed at building up its own life. Great strength is required to push its way through the soil, which can be associated with a more determined, stubborn nature at this phase.

A door in the north-east can make the occupants more susceptible to outside influences, as a door here allows this sharp, piercing kind of energy, similar to a craggy rock, to enter the premises. Of all the eight directions this position is considered the least favourable.

The Chi energy of the north-east supports activities like physical exercise, games and play. This could include an exercise room, a room for competitive games, such as pool or cards, and a children's playroom. In a building, the north-east segment will provide a motivating, competitive atmosphere.

White is the colour that most closely represents the Chi energy of the north east. This time it is a brilliant white, rather like snow-peaked mountains. This shade of white should create a more shiny, sharp, hard atmosphere.

THREE EAST

Five Element	Tree
Symbol	Thunder
Family Member	Eldest Son
Colour	Bright green
Time	Morning

The east segment of a building encourages an active, focused Chi energy. The symbol of thunder gives this Chi energy a great intensity. The eldest son traditionally had the job of providing for the family once his parents retired, and in this sense he is the family's future. The image of the rising sun in the east creates the impression that this is the beginning of the day. The Chi energy of the east is associated with ambition, getting things started and putting ideas into practice. One definition of the influence of this Chi energy is to make a dream a reality. This type of Chi energy is good for a quick start.

Here in the cycle of life the child has grown to young man or woman and is ready to begin his or her career. This is a time of great ambition, and new beginnings. Now the plant's shoots break the ground and the plant experiences rapid growth. This

is a highly active phase, where the young plant develops 39
strength and becomes established.

A door to the east of the centre of a building would be particularly favourable for young people. In particular, this would
help them begin a new career or start a new business. Their
lives would tend to be busy and active. In a commercial building, a door in the east would be particularly beneficial for a
new business or one that is still growing.

The east part of a building is particularly well suited for
things that are by nature active, practical and orientated
towards building for the future. Rooms that would be supported by this kind of Chi energy are an office, kitchen or hobby
room. Because the sun energizes this side of the building in the
morning, this would also be a good location for a breakfast
room. A bedroom in the east would be helpful if the occupants
wish their lives to be more busy, if they are engaged in starting
a new business or building up their careers.

Bright green is the closest colour to this type of Chi energy.
The shade of green is lively and vibrant. Ideally, it would stimulate feelings of growth, freshness and vitality. This green can
often be found on new leaves on a tree or plant.

FOUR SOUTH-EAST

Five Element	Tree
Symbol	Wind
Family Member	Eldest daughter
Colour	Dark green or blue
Time	Mid morning

The south-east part of a building has busy, active Chi energy,
but now the Chi energy is less focused and less sharp than the
Chi energy in the east. The symbol of wind is persistent, has a
great power, but is less aggressive and dramatic than thunder.

Similarly, the eldest daughter is more gentle than the eldest son. This Chi energy encourages orderly and harmonious devel- opment.

At this phase in the cycle of life a person is more mature and making more harmonious progress in their life. The plant now continues its growth, also entering a more mature phase.

A door in the south-east part of a building will also be beneficial for young people. Similar to the east, it encourages activity and is favourable for people beginning a new career or starting their own business. However, the energy here would tend to be more mature and less aggressive. It would help the occupants develop their lives harmoniously. One extra benefit is that a door in this part of the home could enhance aspects of the occupants' lives that relate to communication, as wind represents communication through nature by spreading seeds.

Activities that require an atmosphere that encourages communication, creativity and persistence will work well if they are situated to the south-east of the centre of a building. Rooms could include a kitchen, office and studio. A bedroom in the south-east will also help the occupants develop their careers or business, but in a more gentle manner.

Dark green is closest to the Chi energy of the south-east. A more established, darker green than the vibrant bright green of the east. Dark green represents leaves in more mature stages of growth. This shade of green would ideally create a more established, older atmosphere. At the same time this colour is a shade that instils feelings of growth and vitality. Blue can also be associated with this Chi energy.

Five element	Fire
Symbol	Fire
Family member	Middle daughter
Colour	Purple
Time	Midday

The part of a building that is south of the centre will have Chi energy that is associated with fire, passion and brilliance. Like a candle in the night this energy tends to shine. The character of the middle daughter is outgoing, extrovert and sociable. If the Chi energy in this part of a building moves well, the occupants can expect fame and social popularity.

In the cycle of life this phase represents middle age, when our man or woman has reached a time to enjoy some success and become well-known if the earlier phases were positive. This is the time when our plant comes into flower. Bright and colourful, the plant is highly visible and makes an impression.

A door in the south part of a building will help the occupants become well-known, or even famous, as fire Chi energy is bright and easily noticed. Being stimulated by this fiery, radiant Chi energy, one would expect people living here to have an active social life. This position for a door would also be favourable for stimulating the mind. At the same time, the south has a very active, hot and almost explosive quality. As a result of this, the occupants can feel more argumentative, sometimes leading to separation.

The south of a building is well-suited to social, outgoing, activities. A room designed for parties and entertaining would be supported by the Chi energy found in the south. In addition, south of a building is helpful for stimulating intelligence. For this reason a room in the south can make a good study. Similarly, a bedroom in the south could also benefit a young student. However, the Chi energy of the south is passionate and intense. It may therefore be difficult to concentrate for long periods or to sleep well in the south. This area is highly energetic, although less focused than in the east and south east segments. It is particularly helpful for the occupants to achieve success as a result of being highly visible.

Purple is the colour considered best to represent the Chi energy of the south. It is the shade of purple found at the root of a flame. It is important that the hue of purple chosen instils feelings of passion, excitement and heat.

TWO SOUTH-WEST

Five element	Soil
Symbol	Earth
Family member	Mother
Colour	Black
Time	Afternoon

South-west from the centre of a home, the Chi energy will be more settled and slow. The atmosphere here is more conducive to consolidation and careful, methodical progress. This creates a more cautious environment. The family member is the mother, which can give this Chi energy an influence that encourages family harmony. This part of the home is associated with the mother or the eldest woman in the family.

In the cycle of life the man or woman has reached a more settled phase. This is the time when they are more orientated towards family harmony. By now they may have grandchildren and wish to spend more time with their family. The plant has finished growing and its fruit is becoming sweeter.

A door in the south-west is along the same axis as the northeast in the standard chart. The three soil numbers 8, 5, and 2 are all in a line in which the flow of energy is less stable. These all belong to the element of soil and therefore Chi energy moving along this axis does not need to transform itself into another element of Chi energy. For this reason Chi energy is able to move back and forth through these areas quickly. Although the Chi energy in the south-west is of quite a different nature, it also carries the same changeable nature as Chi energy of the north-east. For this reason a door in the south-west is considered to make it harder to maintain good health.

The south-west of a building is most suited to more settled, homely activities. A family room, crafts or television room would work well here. In a building the segment to the south-west of the centre will benefit the occupants in terms of practically making the most of what they already have. The energy here is more slow and steady.

Black is the colour that is most associated with the Chi energy of the south-west. The shade of black is similar to that found in very rich black soil. The energy of the south-west is strongly associated with the mother and earth. Both have the quality of providing nourishment and supporting life. Therefore, the kind of soil that best represents these qualities is dark, almost like a black fertilizer.

SEVEN WEST

Five Element	Metal
Symbol	Lake
Family Member	Youngest daughter
Colour	Red
Time	Early evening

The west segment of a building has the Chi energy associated with the harvest. This makes the west an important area in terms of financial income. Bright red sunsets make this a potentially romantic place in the home. The image of the lake creates

44 a more reflective, deep impression. Among certain Feng Shui schools metal is associated with money (gold and silver being associated with coins). The youngest daughter gives this area a more playful quality that is associated with the pursuit of pleasure.

In the cycle of life our man or woman has reached an age where they are ready to retire. It is time to relax and enjoy the fruits of their hard work. In the same phase the plant is ready for harvest. The farmer or the rest of nature benefits from the fruits of the plant.

A door to the west of the centre of a building can be beneficial for money and romance. Traditionally, in the orient, this would also be the ideal position for the door to a Geisha house. The idea being that the west relates to romance, pleasure, play and young women, all encompassed within the characteristics of the Chi energy of the west. A door to the west is generally good to encourage a more settled, gentle flow of Chi energy. For a commercial building a door in the west is better for a business that is already established, rather than one that is new or trying to grow, as the west represents the end of the working day.

The type of energy found in the west of a building is ideally suited to the pursuit of pleasure, romance or money. Rooms that would benefit from being in the west of a home are a dining room, a room to entertain or relax in the evenings. A bedroom in the west could lead to a preoccupation with pleasure and a loss of motivation.

Red is the colour chosen to describe the Chi energy of the west. The hue of red is similar to a beautiful red sunset. It should bring out feelings of romance, joy and contentment. At the same time there is a solid appearance associated with metal.

Five Element	Metal
Symbol	Heaven
Family member	Father
Colour	Silver white
Time	Late evening

The Chi energy of the north-west part of a building is associated with leadership, organization and planning ahead. The symbol of heaven gives this Chi energy dignity, wisdom and a superior image. The father adds an authority, respect and responsibility to this part of the building. The north-west of a building has a specific influence on the father, an elder male, or the main wage earner of either sex in the family.

At this stage in the cycle of life the man or woman has been through the whole cycle and is therefore in a position to help others through the earlier phases. This puts them in a position where they have the experience and wisdom to offer. The plant meanwhile has reached the phase where it is being stored to last for the rest of the year. It is a process that is focused on planning ahead for the future. For this reason the north-west part of a building is associated with planning ahead and organization, as well as leadership and wisdom.

The occupants of a building with the main door in the north-west will find it easier to cultivate dignity and respect. This would be helpful for those on the way to some kind of leadership position in their career. Their progress would be slower than those inspired by the Chi energy of the east or south-east. In a commercial building a door in the north-west would encourage success through careful planning and the ability to gain the respect and trust of their clients which would support financial and material success.

Chi energy in the north-west part of a building is ideal for activities that require organization and planning. An office, study, library or bedroom would all suit this type of atmosphere. A bedroom in the north-west would be most suited to the parents. It could help them take care of their family. In a commercial building the north-west is the ideal location for the chairman of a company.

Silvery white is the colour that is closest to the kind of energy in the north-west. Similar to the way someone's hair can give them an air of being dignified, wise and distinguished when it turns silver, this colour should create a similar impression.

FIVE CENTRE

Five element	Soil
Symbol	None
Family member	None
Colour	Yellow
Time	None

The Chi energy of the centre carries the greatest power. It is changeable and has two great extremes of power: productive and destructive. The central Chi energy should ideally also have gathering power. This needs a stable environment. I generally advise occupants to keep the centre part of their building as empty as possible. The nature of this Chi energy is such that it needs more open space. The Chi energy of the centre mixes with all the eight directions.

A hall and landing are ideal in the centre of a building.

The colour of this central Chi energy is yellow. Yellow has the ability to mix well with all the other colours. Ideally it would bring out a feeling of being in the centre of things.

In the Form School of Feng Shui the properties of these eight directions are often simplified into nine squares arranged in the same way as the magic square. This is known as the Ba Gua. Each square is assigned an aspect of your life. These are: north – career; north-east – knowledge; east – family; south-east – wealth; south – fame; south-west – relationships; west – children, and north-west – helpful people. The centre square is known as Tai Chi and sometimes assigned the aspect of health.

There are also other interpretations of how Chi energy moves through a building and a variety of opinions on how to interpret the traditional practice of Feng Shui in this respect. To avoid confusion my advice is to thoroughly study one method, then to research other styles and make your own comparisons.

In this chapter I have described how a building can be divided into eight directions and how each of these eight directions has its own particular movement of Chi energy which will be supportive of specific activities. In addition, the way Chi energy moves in each of the eight directions will determine which kind of room would benefit most from that particular movement of Chi energy. It is also necessary to examine how the basic features of a building, such as the location of the main entrance, will affect the flow of Chi energy through the building.

USING THE COMPASS TO ALIGN THE EIGHT DIRECTIONS

To find out how the Chi energy moves through your home, the grid with eight directions needs to be laid over a floor plan of your living or working space. You will need a compass, protractor, ruler, pencil and paper. The compass needs to be the kind that has an outer dial that can be rotated to take compass bearings. These are typically available in shops that specialize in camping and hiking equipment. (A protractor is a round perspex disk with 360 degrees marked on it, commonly available from stationery retailers).

For simplicity I will refer to houses, apartments, offices, shops, restaurants or any other type of covered space as buildings. If you own or rent only part of a larger building, to begin with, you only need to consider that part of the building that is yours.

First make a floor plan to scale of the space you wish to assess. Take the basic measurements of each room and convert them into a convenient scale. For example, 1 metre equals 1 centimetre. So if you measure a room to be 4.5 metres by 3.8 metres, you would then draw a rectangle on your plan 4.5 centimetres by 3.8 centimetres. Draw each room until you have completed that floor of your building. If you have more than one floor continue to draw separate plans for each floor. If you live in an apartment just draw that apartment.

Next add the doors and windows. If you are not measuring their size and position try to draw them in proportion to the room. When you have your basic floor plan, the next task is to find the centre of your building. Remember when I write 'your building' I am referring only to the space you own, rent or occupy. This could be a house, office or apartment. Later you can assess the whole building including the common areas and other apartments. The easiest shapes are a rectangle, square, circle or octagon. The centre can simply be found by drawing diagonal lines between opposing corners or opposite points on a circle (see Figure 11). These are all considered favourable shapes in Feng Shui.

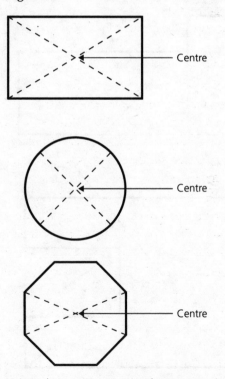

Fig 11 The easiest shapes are a rectangle, square, circle or octagon

More complicated is a building that is an L-shape, or some other irregular shape. For these shapes the simplest method of finding the centre of the area is to break it down to two or more rectangles. Then draw a line between the centres of each rectangle. Compare the size of the rectangles and mark a point along this line in proportion to the size of the rectangles. The mark should be closer to the centre of the larger rectangle (see Figure 12). If you wish to calculate the centre of a complicated shape accurately this information can be found in a geometry book. Another method is to draw the shape of your building's floor plan to scale on a piece of card. Cut out the card and use a needle to find the centre of gravity. Once the card balances on the

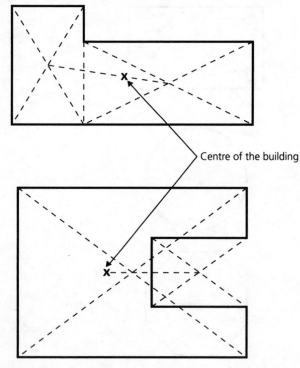

Centre of the building

Fig 12 Finding the centre of a complicated or L-shaped room

needle, pierce the card. The hole will mark the centre of the building.

Once the floor plan is complete and the centre of the building known, we can mark magnetic north on the drawing. Take a compass and point it directly at one of the walls. Walk around your home keeping your compass pointing towards the same wall. The needle of the compass may change direction as you do this. Things made of iron or steel will alter the magnetic field. Many electrical appliances, especially those that have transformers, will create their own magnetic field. Steel beams, pipes or water tanks can be concealed in a building and may

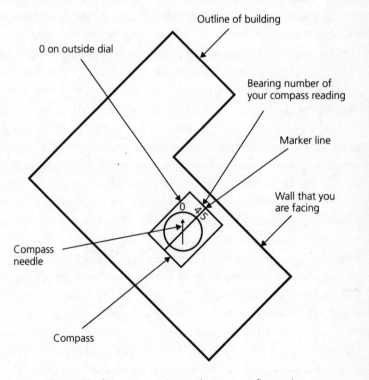

Fig 13 Finding magnetic north on your floor plan

distort your compass readings. I always check several areas of a building, including outside of the building, until I am sure I have a consistent compass reading. Once you are confident you have a consistent reading, whilst holding the compass facing the wall, turn the outside dial of your compass until 0 lines up with the point of your needle. This is north. The marker line on your compass will now be lined up with a number on the dial of your compass (see Figure 13). This number is the bearing that will be used to draw magnetic north on the floor plan.

To mark magnetic north on the floor plan, place the centre of a protractor over the centre of your floor plan. Turn the protractor until the same number that you took from the compass is facing the wall you used to take your compass reading. The number 0 on your protractor will now be facing the same direction on your floor plan as the needle of your compass in your building. Make a mark next to the 0 on your protractor, and draw a line from the centre of your floor through this mark. This line will be pointing towards magnetic north on your plan.

Figure 14 shows you the layout of the eight directions. North, east, south, and west are each wedges of **30** degrees, whereas, north-east, south-east, south-west, and north-west are each **60** degree wedges. Many schools of Feng Shui divide the eight directions into eight equal wedges of 45 degrees. Moreover, when using the eight directions to calculate the effect of someone with a certain basic number, moving in a particular direction, at a specific time, the Feng Shui practitioner will also need to take into account the influence of the twelve animals. These, like the twelve hours on a clock face, are divided into twelve equal segments of 30 degrees. See the outside ring on figure 15. To help synchronize the twelve animals and the eight directions some schools of Feng Shui began to arrange the eight directions into four segments of 30 degrees and four segments of 60 degrees (see Figure 15). This is the method that I have the most

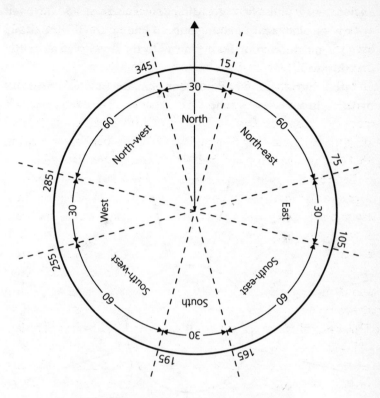

Fig 14 The layout of the eight directions

experience with. A small space is left in the centre of the grid which represents the central Chi energy of 5.

This grid with eight directions can now be drawn over the floor plan, making sure that north on the grid lines up with north on your floor plan. Another method is to draw the grid with eight directions on a piece of tracing paper, then place this over your floor plan. Alternatively, you can draw out the grid on a plain piece of paper and photocopy it onto a transparent sheet. This is a common process for making transparencies for overhead projectors and available at most copy centres. The transparency with the eight directions can then be laid over your floor plan, again making sure to line up the line pointing towards north on your floor plan with the line pointing north on your grid.

With the grid laid over your floor plan, the first feature of the building to assess is its shape.

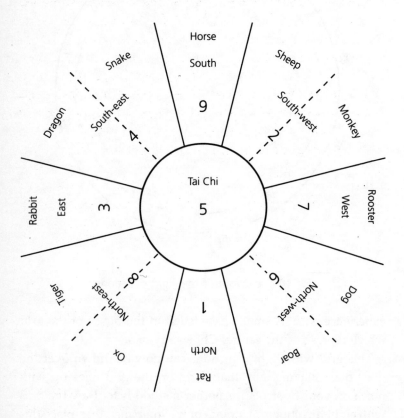

Fig 15 The twelve animals and the eight directions

THE SHAPE OF A BUILDING

A rectangle is the most common shape for a building. This is considered ideal in Feng Shui. However, if it is long and narrow the occupants are expected to find it harder to live a well-balanced life. A long, narrow building will tend to mostly occupy a few areas of the grid, leaving others relatively empty. The areas of the grid that are filled by the floor plan will be well represented in the occupants' lives, whereas those areas that are not filled by the floor plan could be missing from the occupants' lives (see Figure 16). In this example the south-west and north-east mostly fill the floor plan.

A square or a building close to a square will tend to fill the grid evenly and is considered beneficial.

A circle or octagon are more unusual shapes, but should be equally auspicious.

Many houses, apartments or offices are irregular shapes. They fall into two types: a) those with parts missing, and b) those with extensions. A missing part is an indentation that is less than half the length of the building, whereas an extension is where part of the building sticks out. To qualify as an extension it would have to be less than half the length of the building (see Figure 17).

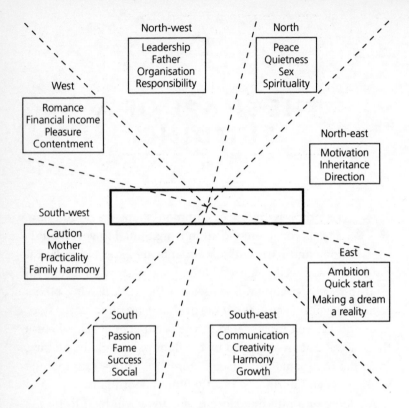

Fig 16 A long, narrow building will tend to occupy a few areas of the grid, leaving others relatively empty

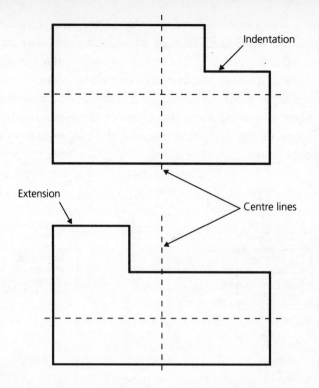

Fig 17 Buildings with a missing part or an extension

Buildings with a small extension will enhance and accentuate
the movement of Chi energy in that part of the building. A large
extension can exaggerate the Chi energy of that area too much,
causing the movement of Chi energy to become unbalanced.
There are no rules or formulae to this. Whether an extension is
too large is a matter of judgement. My advice is to try to find out
how the occupants have developed their lives since moving in.
For example, if the building has an extension in the south-west,
the Chi energy associated with the mother or the eldest woman
would be strengthened. If you were unsure whether this extension was too large, one assessment would be to find out if the

mother's position in the family was too strong and overbearing. If the family's relationship was an unhappy one due to the mother's dominance, it would be safe to assume that the extension in the south-west was too large for this building.

As a simple guide, listed below are the main influences of extensions or missing areas in particular directions of a building. Figure 18 shows an example of a building with an extension to the north.

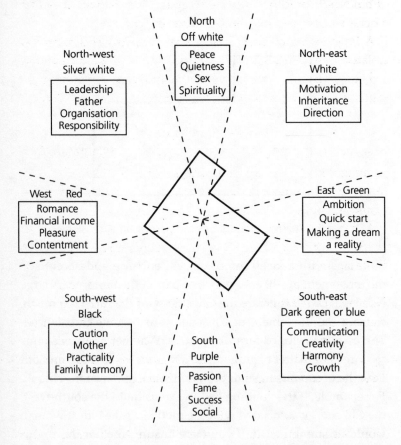

North
Off white
Peace
Quietness
Sex
Spirituality

North-west
Silver white
Leadership
Father
Organisation
Responsibility

North-east
White
Motivation
Inheritance
Direction

West   Red
Romance
Financial income
Pleasure
Contentment

East   Green
Ambition
Quick start
Making a dream
a reality

South-west
Black
Caution
Mother
Practicality
Family harmony

South
Purple
Passion
Fame
Success
Social

South-east
Dark green or blue
Communication
Creativity
Harmony
Growth

Fig 18 An example of a building with an extension to the north

NORTH

A moderate extension in the north would create an atmosphere that tends to make the occupants more interested in spirituality. It could make their lives more quiet and peaceful. They may find greater independence in this building. Generally, this type of building would be more suited to an older person. It can be a beneficial shape for fertility and having children.

A large extension may lead to the occupants becoming too isolated. They could harm themselves by becoming involved in a sexual scandal or they might be infected by a sexually transmitted disease. Their lives may become too quiet.

NORTH-EAST

A small extension in the north-east part of a building would stimulate the Chi energy associated with motivation, a clear sense of direction and hard work. However, no extension would be preferable.

A large extension can cause the north-east Chi energy to overwhelm the building. This sharp, piercing Chi energy can make the movement of Chi energy through the home unstable and unpredictable. In this school of Feng Shui, a large extension in the north-east is thought to lead to misfortune and allow the occupants to be too susceptible to outside influences. A large extension in the north-east can also lead to the occupants having too great a desire for material things and becoming greedy. It may also create problems with inheritance.

EAST

A small extension to the east can be favourable in terms of the occupants' careers and business. With an extension to the east the occupants will tend to be busy, energetic and active. This is more suited to younger people who are actively engaged in building up their lives. In a family, this would be particularly favourable to the eldest son.

A large extension to the east may make the occupants too hectic and create an atmosphere in which it is hard to relax. In addition, the occupants may be tempted to rush too quickly in their desire to succeed and fail.

SOUTH-EAST

A minor extension in the south-east of a building can help the occupants develop their lives harmoniously. This extension could also help stimulate a movement of Chi energy that encourages active life. This would help growth in terms of the occupants' career and business. In a family, this would be favourable for a daughter, especially in terms of marriage. Generally, this shape would be beneficial for prosperity.

Too large an extension in the south-east can lead to over-activity. This in itself can lead to ill health.

SOUTH

A modest extension to the south may encourage fame, public recognition and success. This would help self-promotion. In addition, the occupants of a building with this shape may find that they are more passionate, outgoing and have a busy social life, particularly if the occupants are involved in public affairs.

A large extension can lead to unrealistically high expectations, resulting in disappointment. Too great an influence of Chi energy in the south may lead to excessive passions leading to arguments and separation. Some occupants could find it hard to stay at home in such a building.

A small extension in the south-west of a building can help encourage family harmony and influence the occupants in a way that makes them more practical and methodical.

Too big an extension can create a powerful flow of Chi energy that supports the mother or eldest woman of the household. This can make her more dominant, to the detriment of the rest of the family. This shape is sometimes called a widow's house, as the energy of the wife becomes too strong.

In addition, the occupants could become over-cautious and find it harder to make decisions. The father of the family might lose his enthusiasm to work.

WEST

A moderate extension in the west can be advantageous for financial income and be helpful for occupants seeking to arrange loans. This building could also be beneficial for marriage, particularly for female occupants. A building with this shape can be supportive for entertaining.

A large extension to the west of a building may lead to the occupants' loss of money, along with too great a preoccupation with the pursuit of pleasure. Although this would affect everyone in the family, younger females would be influenced most.

NORTH-WEST

A modest extension in the north-west can be beneficial for the occupants with respect to steadily building up their careers. It is advantageous for planning ahead, having a clear head and developing a fair sense of justice. This shape of building will be supportive to the father or breadwinner of the family. This person could behave more responsibly and take the family's needs seriously.

Too big an extension in the north-west may result in the father, or the main wage earner, becoming too powerful, dominant and self-assured. This could lead to a harmful arrogance.

The following is a simple description of the effect of a missing space in each of the eight directions. Figure 19 shows the example of a building with a missing space to the north.

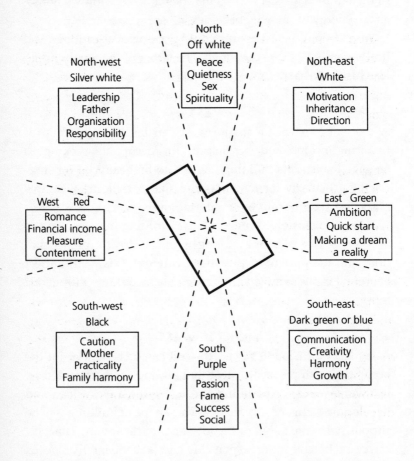

Fig 19 An example of a building with a missing space to the north

A missing space in the north of a building would create an atmosphere that tends to reduce the occupants' sexual vitality or even result in ill health affecting reproductive organs. It is less likely that the occupants of this shape of building would have children. It could also lead to a loss of financial income and possible loss of the good will of employees.

NORTH-EAST

A small missing space in the north-east part of a building can be advantageous, although none is preferable. A large missing space could lead to the occupants losing the desire to work. In addition, a large missing space can lead to difficulties in pregnancy, and the children in such a home could become weak.

EAST

A missing space to the east may also cause children growing in this building to be weak or encounter difficulties. This would affect the eldest son in particular. This might also have a negative effect on the occupants' nervous system.

SOUTH-EAST

A missing space in the south-east of a building can result in the occupants losing power to develop their lives harmoniously, and their career or business could weaken. The occupants may also become lazy. In terms of health this could affect the intestines and weaken the occupants' resistance to colds. A large missing space in the south-east is considered to lead to misfortune for the occupants and is not auspicious for the family's destiny.

SOUTH

A missing area to the south could make the occupants more vulnerable to law suits and public prosecution. In addition, they could be more susceptible to eye, heart and, in women, breast illnesses.

SOUTH-WEST

A missing area in the south-west of a building can weaken the mother or the eldest woman in the family. This situation could also make it harder to achieve family harmony. The occupants of a building with this shape may become more prone to illnesses affecting their stomachs.

WEST

A missing space in the west may lead to a lack of contentment. This would particularly affect the youngest daughter or the youngest woman in a family. A woman living in a building with this shape could find herself living alone, unable to find a romantic partner. The occupants of this building might experience illnesses of the lungs. A large missing area in the west can lead to a loss of property and assets.

NORTH-WEST

A missing area in the north-west can weaken the energy of the father or main wage earner of the family. He could also be more prone to mental disorders. This shape is also known as a widow's home, as the power of the husband becomes weak.

Once the influence of the shape of a building has been established, you can start to assess how well the features of your building are suited to each direction on the grid. To help, I have listed in the next chapter some of the key points with respect to doors and water.

THE FEATURES OF A BUILDING

DOORS

Any entrance, whether it be a gate to a piece of land, a door to a building or a door to a room, influences the flow of Chi energy. Often in Feng Shui a door is referred to as a gate. Although Chi energy can flow through walls, it moves more easily through a doorway, particularly as the Chi energy is carried along by the movement of people. A door that is used by people frequently will have a bigger influence on the flow of Chi energy throughout a building than a door that is used occasionally.

The size of a door will influence the movement of Chi energy. A door that is comfortably larger than the largest occupant of the building will ensure that the occupants and their own Chi energy field can pass through entrances without congestion. A large door will also encourage Chi energy to move into and out of the building. However, this is only desirable if the door is located in a beneficial direction from the centre of the building or your apartment.

The way a door opens will also affect the flow of Chi energy. A door that opens into an open space will allow Chi energy to flow more freely. If a door opens into a narrow corridor, confined space or into a wall, the Chi energy can become congested, with the result that it does not move easily.

To determine the effect a door has on a building and the occupants of that building, look at the floor plan and decide in which of the eight directions the door is located. Make sure that you have found the centre of the building and that you have placed the centre of the eight directions over the centre of your floor plan. Align north on the drawing of the eight directions with north on the floor plan and see in which of the eight directions the door appears. The door will then tend to encourage the flow of that particular Chi energy into the building. For example, if the door is located to the south-east from the centre of a building, this door will encourage Chi energy from the south-east to flow into the building. To decide how this influences the occupants of the building, look up the qualities of the Chi energy from the south-east in chapter five.

An additional consideration is the direction the door faces. For example, you may have a building with a door to the east of the centre of a building, however, the door itself actually faces south. The direction of the door has a smaller influence than the position. The principle is the same. If the position of a door is east from the centre of the building, it encourages those qualities associated with Chi energy from the east. At the same time the door faces south, so it also encourages Chi energy from the south to enter. This adds the properties of Chi energy from the south to the influence of the door. As the influence of the direction of the door is minor compared to the position of the door I suggest you just consider the position of the door.

To help understand the influence of a door I have written a description of the key points for each direction.

A door to the north from the centre of a building will encourage water Chi energy to enter the building. Generally the Chi energy is too cold for a door or entrance. This Chi energy can make the occupants' lives more quiet. A door in the north is good for hiding. People living or working in such a building could find themselves becoming isolated. It could also increase feelings of insecurity or worry.

NORTH-EAST

A door in the north-east, from the centre, is the least desirable position. A door in the north-east is said to make the occupants more susceptible to negative influences from spirits. The Chi energy from the north-east is considered cold and piercing. This would make the building less comfortable. In addition, a door in the north-east part of a building can cause the movement of Chi energy to change suddenly. This may make the fortunes of the occupants susceptible to changes. A door in the north-east is not considered beneficial for health. It can also lead to difficulties in producing a child.

EAST

A door that is located to the east from the centre of a building can be particularly helpful for young people. Energized by the rising sun, the east is a position that helps create a bright future. This influence is supportive to the occupants' careers and their business. It is the direction that is most likely to lead to quick progress. A door in the east is ideal for someone starting a new business. Because a door to the east is beneficial for business, getting something new started and a bright future, it is very good for the entrance to a commercial building, particularly if it is a new business.

SOUTH-EAST

A door positioned south-east from the centre of a building will bring in Chi energy that encourages the occupants' lives to develop harmoniously. Chi energy from the south-east will help the occupants to be more creative. Because Chi energy from the south-east is associated with communication, a door in the south-east can lead the occupants to have good connections socially and in their business. A door in the south-east can also help the occupants develop their careers or businesses, although not as quickly or intensely as a door in the east.

SOUTH

A door south from the centre of a building will allow more of the kind of Chi energy that creates fame and public recognition to enter. The occupants of such a building may find success through becoming well-known in their field. Chi energy from the south would help the occupants develop intelligence. This would be advantageous for students. In a house, a door in the south could lead the occupants to be more social and such a house could be good for parties. In a commercial property, a door to the south could lead to success through a good reputation. Oxford Street in London runs east to west. The shops on the north side of Oxford Street have their entrances facing south and in most cases the entrances are located in the south of the building. When compared to the shops on the south side, whose doors are in the north, significantly more of the shops with their doors in the south have enjoyed long-term success, fame and good reputations. Another consideration with a door in the south is that it brings in a fiery, hot energy. This intense energy can make the occupants lives more stressful, argumentative and eventually end up in separation.

SOUTH-WEST

A door in the south-west part of a building, being on the opposite side to the north-east, is not favourable. This Chi energy also leads to the changeable, unstable movements of Chi energy. A door in the south-west is considered particularly harmful for the occupants' health. The Chi energy of the south-west is not fast and can lead to slow progress in terms of the occupants' careers or business.

WEST

A door to the west of the centre of a building is beneficial for romance and pleasure. Traditionally, it was considered the ideal location for the door in a geisha house. A door here would tend to favour young women. The Chi energy of the west is represented by the setting sun and this quality of Chi energy is more settled. By bringing more of this west Chi energy into the building, the occupants can feel more content. This feeling of contentment may also, however, lead to the occupants feeling less motivated. A door in the west may help financial income, although it could also lead to excessive expenditure.

NORTH-WEST

A door situated to the north-west of the centre of a building will place the occupants in a position of respect and dignity. A door here can make it easier for the occupants of this building to win the trust of their community. North-western Chi energy brings in the qualities associated with leadership, organization and responsibility. These characteristics favour the parents of the family and, in particular, the main wage earner. Traditionally, having a door in the north-west from the centre of a building would be ideal for the father of the family. It would place him in a more powerful position.

Traditionally, the site of a water well was considered of great importance to the family's health, prosperity and spiritual well-being. The well brought life itself into the home, in the form of drinking water. At the same time, water is associated with the spirits of the occupant's ancestors. If the ideal place for a well, relative to the centre of a building, could be found, this water would have the power to bring great fortune to everyone in that particular building.

It is less common in this age for a building to have its own drinking water well, so water would include the following: the main water pipe to a building; a bathroom; a toilet; the kitchen sink; a pond; a swimming pool; a fountain; an aquarium, and other indoor water features. Large water features nearby should also be taken into consideration. This includes rivers, lakes and the sea.

In many schools of Feng Shui water is said to represent money. For this reason it is very common to find an aquarium in an oriental business, such as a Chinese restaurant. In the Compass system of Feng Shui the location of any water is important.

It is essential that the water remains fresh. If the water becomes dirty or stagnant, it can begin to have a negative effect on the flow of Chi energy.

The next part of assessing a building is to locate the places where the water is and to then decide what effect water will have on the occupants' lives in that particular part of the building. To do this it is necessary to calculate in which direction from the centre of the building the water is located. I have written a description of the effect of water in each of the eight directions.

Any water to the north of the centre of a building will be in its own element of water. In this respect water here would have a neutral effect. However, the Chi energy of the north tends to be cold, quiet and still. This can make it hard to get rid of dampness, moisture or humidity. For this reason, the north part of a building would not be the best place for a bathroom. Constant dampness in the north could lead to frequent illnesses.

NORTH-EAST

The north-east part of a building or a north-easterly direction from a building, are considered the least desirable direction to have water. Water Chi energy does not mix well with the five element Chi energy of the north-east, which is soil. In the five element theory soil Chi energy will destroy water Chi energy, if metal Chi energy is not sufficient. Of all the kinds of water features, a bathroom or toilet would be the most harmful to the occupants if located in the north-east. Because the north-east is a direction where Chi energy changes quickly, sudden movements of water, such as flushing a toilet, will add to these unstable movements of Chi energy. This can result in the occupants experiencing sudden, unexpected changes in their lives. When in this position, a toilet and bathroom are considered to lead to poor health.

EAST

The element of water Chi energy supports the tree Chi energy to the east. Generally, water in the east is considered favourable. This is an excellent location for a kitchen, pond, swimming pool, fountain, or indoor water feature such as an aquarium. The east would also be an advantageous place for the main water pipe to enter a site or building. As water here builds up the east Chi energy, the occupants could benefit in terms of their careers, activity and the ability to make their dreams a reality. Opinions vary with respect to whether a bathroom or toilet should be located in the east part of a building. My own opinion is that a toilet to the east is less harmful than to the south, south-west, west, north or north-east. However, a lot depends on the toilet or bathroom itself. A toilet that has no windows, and therefore no exposure to natural light or fresh air, is a much greater problem than a toilet that receives sunlight and has a window that can be opened. It is common, in apartments and modern houses, to locate the toilet and bathroom in places where they are not next to an outside wall. Without light and fresh air, it is much more difficult to avoid a build-up of stagnant Chi energy. This is made even worse when the bathroom is damp and cluttered. In this situation the toilet and bathroom will have a negative effect wherever they are.

SOUTH-EAST

Chi energy to the south-east is also associated with tree Chi energy. Again, water Chi energy will support the tree Chi energy of the south-east part of a building. In this direction water will build up Chi energy that helps the occupants in terms of communication, creativity and the ability to develop their lives harmoniously. The effect will be more gentle when compared with placing water in the east. The south-east is suitable for all the types of water features listed above, with the same considerations with regard to a bathroom or toilet.

SOUTH

The Chi energy of water is the opposite to the Chi energy of fire, found in the southern part of a building. If there is not sufficient tree Chi energy present, the water Chi energy will destroy the Chi energy in the south. So the water features listed previously are generally considered harmful when located to the south.

The occupants of such a building could be more prone to law suits against them, loss of reputation and poor health. In particular, this may affect the occupants' eyes and heart.

SOUTH-WEST

The Chi energy in the south-west is associated with the soil Chi energy. Soil Chi energy has the ability to destroy water Chi energy if there is not enough metal Chi energy present. That is why it is not recommended to have a water feature to the south-west. In oriental medicine, water Chi energy, which is associated with a person's kidneys, is considered to be the source of Chi energy. Water Chi energy provides the vital force for all other elements of Chi energy. When water is located south-west from the centre of a building the Chi energy that the water brings to the building is destroyed by the soil Chi energy of the south-west. The occupants of such a building can suffer severe illnesses.

WEST

The Chi energy to the west of the centre of a building is considered metal Chi energy. Water in the west part of a building can create the effect of drawing the metal Chi energy of the west. In my opinion this is most likely if the bathroom or toilet are situated to the west. Once this is the case, the occupants of the building are more susceptible to financial losses and difficulties in finding romance.

NORTH-WEST

Water in the north-west will have a similar effect as in the west, although water coming into the building could work harmoniously with the Chi energy of the north-west. I would not recommend a toilet or bathroom here. This could lead to a weakness in terms of organization, responsibility and planning ahead.

74   The same process of examining the nature or type of influence of a feature and then assessing how this will affect the Chi energy of each of the eight directions can be applied to other features within your building. Other features that I would typically consider inside a building would include a fireplace (fire Chi energy), a safe for money (metal Chi energy) and tall plants (tree Chi energy). Stairs and windows will have a similar influence to the door.

THE DIRECTION AND TIMING OF A MOVE

From my experience of researching how my clients' lives have changed since moving their homes or businesses, one of the biggest influences is the timing and direction of the move. Imagine moving a tree. The first task is to take it out of its existing soil, next to move it in a way that does not harm the tree, then to replant during the best time of year for it to become established in its new environment and finally, to make sure it is planted in the kind of soil that it will thrive in. If all the stages are beneficial for the tree it will thrive in its new location. Human beings are the same. Wherever we live our Chi energy mixes with the Chi energy of our local environment in the same way that a tree's roots learn how to live in the soil that surrounds it.

The local Chi energy influences the movement of our own Chi energy which in turn influences our thoughts, emotions and ideas. I think this partly explains why particular parts of a continent, country or city have pockets where people tend to do the same kind work very successfully. I have read historical books and surveys on the part of London where I live, which is close to Primrose Hill. It is fascinating to see how many well-known writers lived there in a small community during the 1800s. Nearby, the main industry was the manufacture and repair of pianos, further west was an area populated by more wealthy merchants. Presumably, for these communities of people to be successful in a particular vocation over a long period of history, the local Chi energy must have supported those activities.

When we leave one place it is almost as though we literally pull our roots out of the soil. We pull our own Chi energy out of the local Chi energy that we have been used to.

When we move, the direction and timing of that move determine how our own Chi energy can mix with new Chi energy in which we want to plant ourselves. For example, if you and I were to sail across the sea to begin a new life, we would first need to study the tides, the water currents, the direction of the prevailing winds and any local variations. If we did our homework well, we could choose a date and time to begin our journey, so that the wind and water actually carry us to our destination. Should we leave it to chance, the winds and tide might push us back again, or even take us to a completely different destination. By choosing the best time to move in a certain direction we can actually charge up our own Chi energy in a positive way.

Another example is to think how important timing is when planting seeds. By choosing a time when the season and weather are ideal, the seeds will have a much greater opportunity to flourish. In my experience it is the same with human beings. When moving to a new home or workplace, the opportunity is there to actually enhance your life and flourish in the same way as a healthy plant. Unfortunately, by moving in a direction and at a time that does not suit your own Chi energy, like a seed planted in an inappropriate season, you are more likely to wither. If you have dreams of what you want to do with your life, the secret is to plant these dreams at a time, and in a place, that they will grow and flourish into something you can make a reality.

To determine how a move will affect your life, your own Nine Ki Year chart will describe your Chi energy, and the Nine Ki chart of the year will describe what type of Chi energy can be found in each of the eight directions that year. The idea is to assess how the Chi energy of the direction in which you want to move, and the Chi energy you are leaving, influence your own Chi energy. The same principle is applied to find the best month and day to move. The Chi energy of the year will have greatest influence, especially when moving longer distances and moving home or offices. When travelling for a short time, i.e. less than a month, the month and the day have the biggest effect, therefore you should consult an experienced practitioner for advice. To make this chapter easier to understand I will solely concentrate on the influence of the Nine Ki chart for each year.

Some years ago I went to a couple's home to provide Feng Shui advice. He was a lawyer and she was an actress. They were both relatively successful in their home in west London. However, they decided to move to east London. His career really took off, whereas her career stopped altogether. He became a partner in the firm in charge of legal contracts and this department grew at a much faster rate than the other departments. Unfortunately, she did not receive any new offers for her acting and she was finding it hard to write a book she had started. Her misfortune could not be explained by the Feng Shui of the house alone, as her husband's career had improved since moving. When I calculated the influence of the timing and direction of their move to this home from their previous one, I found that the move was particularly favourable for him and harmful for her. In particular, his move east at that time was ideal for building up his business, whereas for her it was destructive towards her career. In this situation there are several solutions. The one she chose helped her complete her book.

The same principle applies to deciding when to renovate or change parts of a house or building. I have clients who extended part of their house, only to find they encountered unexpected difficulties, and others who have made a similar extension to their home and experienced many positive changes in their lives. By calculating the direction of the extension, the time it was built and the occupants' Nine Ki charts I could understand why this happened and make appropriate recommendations.

I will now explain how to calculate: a) the best time to move in a certain direction; b) which direction would help you most in a certain year; c) the effects of moves you made in the past, and d) when to change the flow of Chi energy in a part of a building.

To do this you will need your Nine Ki Year number and the Nine Ki chart for the year in which you want to move. Both of these can be found in Chapter 4. For example, someone who was born after 20:17 (GMT) on 4 February 1963 and before 02:08 (GMT) on 5 February 1964 has the Nine Ki Year number 1. If he or she wants to know the effects of moving after 08:01 (GMT) on 4 February 1998, and before 13:51 (GMT) on 4 February 1999, he or she will need the Nine Ki chart with 2 in the centre position.

The method is the same one you learnt for laying the eight directions over a building. Take a map and mark your home with an X. Draw a line from your home going due north. For now, true north, towards the top of the map is acceptable. Then draw on the eight directions or place your transparency with the eight directions so that the centre is over your home and north on the transparency is aligned with north on your map. Note the direction of your proposed move.

The following are six types of moves that can be harmful. I have placed them in order of importance. The first four can potentially cause the greatest harm.

TOWARDS THE POSITION OF 5

When you move in a direction that moves you towards the position of 5 in the Nine Ki chart for that year, you move in the direction of great power. As this power can work destructively, the risk of moving in this direction is too great. For example, in a year when 2 is in the centre of the Nine Ki chart, the Chi energy of number 5 is in the north-east. Anyone, regardless of their Nine Ki Year number, moving north-east that year will be moving towards the Chi energy of 5 (see Figure 20). In a year when the Chi energy of 5 is in the centre, no one can move towards 5. If your own Nine Ki Year number is 5, moving towards the Chi energy of 5 in a particular year means you are moving in a direction that is both towards 5 and your own Nine Ki Year number. This makes the move potentially more harmful.

The Chi energy represented by 5 is the most powerful form of the nine types of Chi energy. Because of the ability to either be productive or destructive, it is considered dangerous to take the risk of moving into this Chi energy. This move can lead to gradual destruction of someone's health, business or career. It is believed that this process happens slowly as destructive forces begin to build up.

MOVING AWAY FROM 5

Moving in a direction that takes you away from the position of Chi energy 5 in a particular year is travelling away from the power centre. This time, in a year when 2 is in the centre of the Nine Ki chart, anyone, regardless of their Nine Ki Year number,

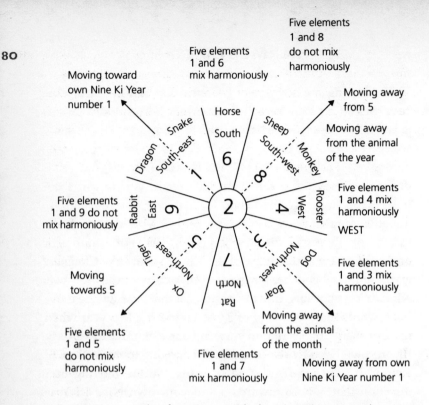

Five elements
1 and 8
do not mix
harmoniously

Five elements
1 and 6
mix harmoniously

Moving toward
own Nine Ki Year
number 1

Moving away
from 5

Moving away
from the animal
of the year

Five elements
1 and 9 do not
mix harmoniously

Five elements
1 and 4 mix
harmoniously

WEST

Moving
towards 5

Five elements
1 and 3 mix
harmoniously

Five elements
1 and 5
do not mix
harmoniously

Moving away
from the animal
of the month

Five elements
1 and 7
mix harmoniously

Moving away from own
Nine Ki Year number 1

Fig 20 An example of someone with the Nine Ki Year number 1
moving in a year when 2 is in the centre

will be moving in a direction that is away from 5 if they move
south-west (see Figure 20). In a year when the Chi energy of 5 is
in the centre, no one can move away from 5. If your own Nine
Ki Year number is 5, moving away from the Chi energy of 5 in a
particular year means you are moving in a direction that is both
away from 5 and away from your own Nine Ki Year number.
This makes the move potentially more harmful.

By moving away from the Chi energy of 5, you are moving
away from this powerful and potentially destructive force. Again,
this is considered dangerous and an unnecessary risk. By moving
away from such a powerful concentration of Chi energy, your

own Chi energy becomes weakened. Such a move could make someone more vulnerable to accidents, injuries and robberies.

Both moving away from or towards 5 will have varying effects depending on where 5 is in that year. For example, moving towards 5 when 5 is in the west will have a different influence to when 5 is in the east. When 5 is in the west this will affect wealth and romance, whereas when 5 is in the east, the influence will affect someone's career.

MOVING TOWARDS YOUR OWN NINE KI YEAR NUMBER

Look at the chart of the year you wish to move. Try to avoid moving towards your own Nine Ki Year number. For example, if someone with the Nine Ki Year number 1 moves south-east in a year when 2 is in the centre of the Nine Ki chart, they are moving towards their own Nine Ki Year number (see Figure 20).

If your own Nine Ki Year number is in the centre of the Nine Ki chart for that year you cannot move in a direction that is towards yourself. Essentially, this move is like trying to push 2 magnets together when both poles have the same charge. By forcing your own Chi energy into a direction that already has the same Chi energy that year, a strong reaction occurs. This can lead to poor health, feelings of always being under great stress and a more confused mental state. Rather than life proceeding smoothly, things that should have been relatively simple often turn out to require much more time and energy than they used to.

MOVING AWAY FROM YOUR OWN NINE KI YEAR NUMBER

Moving away from your own Nine Ki Year number is also considered potentially harmful. Again, look at the chart of the year in which you wish to move, and find your own Nine Ki Year number. For example, in a year when 2 is in the centre of the Nine Ki chart, a person who has the Nine Ki Year number 1 will be moving away from their own Chi energy when they move north-west (see Figure 20). If your own Nine Ki Year number is in the centre of the Nine Ki chart for that year you cannot move in a direction that is away from your own Chi energy.

Moving away from a direction that has the same type of Chi energy as your basic Chi energy is almost like leaving part of yourself behind. People I have met who have made such a move describe it as a loss of confidence. It can lead to feelings of disorientation and an inability to organize their lives properly.

MOVING AWAY FROM
THE ANIMAL OF THE YEAR

To calculate this I need to include the twelve Chinese animals. Figure 21 shows the standard Nine Ki chart with 5 in the centre and the twelve animals in their positions around the Nine Ki chart. The twelve animals always stay in these positions regardless of the year. However, each year one of these animals becomes more active. I have included the appropriate years from 1996 on the chart. For example, in 1990, starting at 09:20 (GMT) on 4 February, the Horse becomes the most active animal for that year. The Horse is always situated in the south, so in 1990 there is an additional concentration of energy in the south. The following year, 1991, the Sheep becomes the most highly-charged animal. The sheep is located to the south-south-west, and therefore this direction has a special concentration of Chi energy. Each year is represented by an animal and at the end of each year the next animal in a clockwise direction becomes the animal to represent that year. So 1992 is the year of the Monkey, 1993 the year of the Rooster, 1994 the year of the Dog, 1995 the year of the Boar, 1996 the year of the Rat, and so on. The years the twelve animals become active do not follow

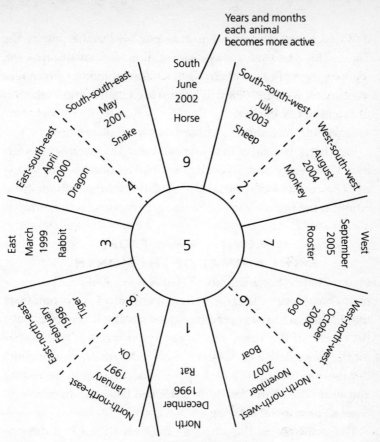

Years and months each animal becomes more active

Note: The Nine Ki numbers will change position each year. Only the twelve animals stay in the same position

Fig 21 The standard Nine Ki chart, with 5 in the centre, and the twelve animals in their positions

the same cycle as the Nine Ki numbers. On Figure 21 the years apply to the twelve animals only.

To move in a direction away from the animal that represents that year is considered to be travelling in a direction that leads to a deficiency of energy. For example, 1998 is the year of the Tiger. The Tiger is always situated in the east-north-east. Anyone, regardless of their Nine Ki Year number, who moves west-south-west in 1998 will be moving in a direction which is deficient in Chi energy.

Travelling in a direction that takes you away from the Chi energy of the animal of that year can lead to a deficiency in your own Chi energy and, in particular, lead to situations breaking up. This could be the break-up of a relationship, separation from a family, the break-down of business negotiations or contracts.

MOVING AWAY FROM
THE ANIMAL OF THE MONTH

Figure 21 also shows the month that is associated with each animal. These never change, so December is always the month of the Rat, January always the month of the Ox, February always the month of the Tiger, and so on. These months do not start on the same date as a western month. Normally they change between the 3rd and 9th of the month, depending on the month and year. The charts for these dates can be found in books on Nine Ki or oriental astrology.

The principle is the same as for moving away from the animal of the year. Anyone moving south in the month of December, regardless of their own Nine Ki Year number, will be moving away from the Rat, the animal of the month. The effect of this move is essentially the same as moving away from the animal of the year, except the influence of such a move is smaller and more temporary.

Finally, to move in a direction that will help improve your life it is important to move towards a number whose Five Element type of Chi energy is in harmony with your own Five Element type of Chi energy. Staying with a year when 2 is in the centre,

I will use the example of a person whose Nine Ki Year number is 1, to find out which directions will be beneficial for that person in that year (see Figure 20).

Look at the Nine Ki chart with 2 in the middle as I describe the effects of a move in each direction. The numbers are in different positions to the standard chart, however the directions always stay in the same position. North is always at the bottom, east to the left, south at the top and west to the right.

If this imaginary person moves north, he moves away from 6 in the south and towards 7 in the north. The next step is to check the possible dangerous moves. His own Nine Ki Year number is 1, so he is neither moving away from or towards himself. He is not moving towards or away from 5. Let us assume the year is 1998, the year of the Tiger. He is not moving away from the animal of that year. If we assume the month is May, the month of the Snake, he is not moving away from the animal of that month either. So none of the six dangerous directions apply. Someone with the Nine Ki Year chart of 1 has the Chi energy associated with water. When 2 is in the centre position, 7 is in the north. The number 7 has the Five Element Chi energy of metal. Metal and water Chi energy mix harmoniously with each other. I would therefore expect this move to be positive.

Should this person move north-east he will move towards 5, which would be moving in a destructive direction. In such a case, I would not recommend he makes this move or makes any alterations to his building north-east from the centre.

To move east he would move away from 4 and towards 9. He is not moving towards or away from 5, not moving towards or away from his own Nine Ki number (1), not moving away from the animal of that year (Tiger) and not moving away from the animal of the month (Snake). So far, we can assume that for someone with the Nine Ki Year number 1, it would be safe to move east in May of 1998. However, this person will be moving towards 9, which is a Fire element. The number 1, a water element Chi energy, will not mix harmoniously with a fire element Chi energy, so this would not be a desirable move after all.

If this person moved south-east he would move away from 3 and towards 1. As his own Nine Ki Year number is 1 he would be moving towards himself. In addition, this person would be moving away from the animal of that month (May – Snake). This would not be a favourable move.

A move south would involve moving towards 6 and away from 7. He is not moving towards or away from himself, not moving towards or away from 5, not moving away from the animal of the year and he would not be moving away from the animal of the month. As 6 is also associated with the Chi energy of metal, and mixes harmoniously with the water Chi energy of 1, this would therefore be a positive move.

Moving south-west he would move from 5, towards 8. Should he make this move he would be moving away from 5, which could make him more vulnerable to accidents. In addition he moves away from the animal of that year, the Tiger. I would consider this to be an especially harmful move.

To move west he moves away from 9 and towards 4. He is not moving towards or away from himself, not moving towards or away from 5, not moving away from the animal of the year or from the animal of the month. The number 4 is not opposite its position on the standard chart. As 4 is also associated with the Chi energy of tree and mixes harmoniously with the water Chi energy of 1, this would therefore be a positive move.

Moving north-west he will move away from 1 and towards 3. He would therefore be moving away from himself and, in addition, moving away from the monthly animal, Snake, in the south-south-east. This would not be a helpful move.

So a person whose Nine Ki Year number is 1, could move north, south or west in May 1998. Each direction will have a different influence. Read my description of each of the eight directions in chapter 5 to discover what kind of influence each direction will have. In this case he could move north to become more quiet, peaceful, isolated, independent and spiritual. A direction to get away from everything and find solitude, but not beneficial if he is a young person building up his life. South, to be more social, expressive, passionate and, perhaps, well-known or famous. If he is in a relationship, moving south could increase the desire to argue and lead to separation. West may lead to romance, greater financial reward and contentment. There is the chance that once content he could lose motivation and become too keen on his own pleasures. All the effects mentioned above will vary depending on which number is in a particular direction at the time you are moving. You have to consider the nature of that number and then take into consideration which of the eight positions that number is 'sitting in'. This requires lot of experience and practice so, if you wish to be totally sure, I would advise that you seek professional advice.

Depending on what is most important to you in your life, it is possible to find a direction that most closely enhances the kind of Chi energy you need to succeed. Sometime you may need to wait a few years until the best direction becomes available to you.

The following are some basic guidelines for a permanent move from one home to another:

a   The direction you move is from the place you have been sleeping for at least three months to the next destination. It is not the route you choose to get there, but where you are now and your final destination that is used to measure the direction.

b To establish yourself in the new Chi energy, you need to sleep every night in the new location for at least two months, preferably three if the journey is within the same country. Just as a seed will not become established in new soil if you keep pulling it up, humans need a period of time to establish their own roots.

c The bigger the distance you move, the stronger and quicker the effects.

On trips of less than 6 weeks it is possible to find the best month and day, even if the direction for the year is not helpful. I would avoid moving towards or away from 5 and avoid moving towards or away from your own number.

To do this, the principles are the same, except you need to know the dates the months change and the Chi energy of each day.

When considering changes to a building I use the same principle. In my Feng Shui reports I include a choice of exact dates to implement certain recommendations. These recommendations are the things I consider to have a significant effect on the flow of Chi energy. For example, if I am to recommend adding a water feature to the east part of a building I also find which months and dates in a particular year will be most favourable to do this. In some situations, adding a water feature in the east could make the flow of Chi energy less favourable if it was done at the wrong time, for instance when the Nine Ki number 5 is in the east. The saying, 'there is a time and place for everything', makes a lot of sense. Everything we know is made up of time and space. In my opinion just making recommendations based on changing the space leaves the effects of the timing of those changes to chance.

As the year has the greatest influence and as the space of this book is limited, it is sufficient for now to make a chart for the whole year and ignore the influence of the months and days. Imagine you are going to use Feng Shui to change the movement of Chi energy in a building in the year 1997. Use the chart with 3 in the centre for 1997 and place it over the building you are working on. Now examine the numbers in each direction. To begin with, I suggest you solely concentrate on where the Nine Ki number 5 is. In 1997 the Nine Ki number 5 is in the west. Therefore, in 1997 I would not recommend making any changes that significantly change the flow of Chi energy towards 5, in the west part of the building or away from 5 in the east part of a building. For that year you could confine the changes to the other six directions. In the next year, 1998, the chart with 2 in the centre shows that 5 is now in the north-east. In 1998 I would avoid changing the flow of Chi energy in the north-east, towards 5, and the south-west, away from 5.

The key points of this chapter are that each person has the ability to enhance the flow of their own Chi energy by choosing to move in a direction and at a time when their own Chi energy will respond positively to the new Chi energy they move into, as well as the Chi energy they are moving away from. Choosing the kind of Chi energy you move towards and away from, you can charge your own Chi energy in a way that helps your life develop in a particular way.

By now I hope you can measure the direction someone moved from his former home to the current one. Find the correct chart for the year he moved, decide which Nine Ki numbers he moved away from and towards, work out his own Nine Ki Year number and decide what effects this move would have on his life.

FENG SHUI SOLUTIONS

There are two ways to help enhance your life with Feng Shui. The first is to place yourself so that your own Chi energy is being positively influenced by the flow of Chi energy through a building. In practice this is determined by where you sleep, work and sit most of the time. The second is to change the way Chi energy moves through a building with the aim of creating a flow of Chi energy that is more appropriate to the needs of the occupants.

I will begin with advice on where to position yourself.

BEDS

There are three considerations. First, which room to use as a bedroom, secondly, where to place the bed within the bedroom and thirdly, which direction the bed should face. So you could have your bed in the east part of your home, the south part of your bedroom and facing west. The position within the home will have a bigger influence than the position within the bedroom. However, the direction the bed faces has a significant influence. When I refer to the direction a bed faces I mean the direction the top of the occupant's head points towards whilst

they are asleep. A bed that faces east means the top of their
head is pointing east and their feet west.

Each of the eight directions generates a type of Chi energy
that will charge your own Chi energy as you sleep. You can
work this out yourself from the information in chapter 5. The
following is a quick guide.

NORTH

Sleeping north of centre of a home or with the top of your head
pointing north, is ideal for quiet sleep. Letting your Chi energy
be charged by the Chi energy of the north whilst you sleep can
make your life more quiet, peaceful and tranquil. In the orient,
it is sometimes referred to as the death position, as sleeping in
the north, or facing north, is considered ideal close to the time
someone is to die. It calms the Chi energy and enhances the
spiritual nature of their Chi energy. I would not recommend the
north for young people or anyone, regardless of age, who is still
trying to advance their career or expand their business. Neither
would I recommend it for someone who is lonely, as the north
could make them more isolated. Sleeping in the north or facing
north is worth trying temporarily if you have a child who cannot sleep well. In addition the Chi energy of the north is associated with sex, so this position or direction might help restart
dormant sexual activity.

NORTH-EAST

Sleeping in the north-east part of your home or facing north-
east, provides you with a motivating, competitive and sharp
Chi energy. At times this could be helpful for children or even
adults. However, generally, I would not recommend the north-
east for sleep. I have come across a number of people who sleep
in the north-east and are haunted by violent nightmares. These
have subsided once they change the position of their bed. I

would not recommend this position or direction for anyone who is concerned about their health. Placing the children in the north-east can make the parents work harder. I have known families whose children sleep in the north-east and the parents in a weaker position, only to find that the parents' whole lives revolve around their children.

EAST

Sleeping east of the centre of a home or facing east, can be ideal for building up your career or business. This is a particularly favourable position and direction for young people. East can be beneficial for becoming more active, more ambitious and having the ability to put your dreams into practice. Soon after I turned my bed to face east my business increased steadily. See Figure 22 for an example of this ideal placement.

SOUTH-EAST

By sleeping in the Chi energy of the south-east, facing the south-east you could also experience positive developments in your career or business. This influence will be more gentle and lead to more harmonious progress. The Chi energy of the south-east also has a creative nature and can help in terms of communication.

SOUTH

The Chi energy of the south is ideal for passion, intelligence and fame. However, this kind of Chi energy is almost the opposite of sleep. The south represents the middle of the day, whereas sleep takes place at night. Occupants sleeping here might find themselves lying awake thinking. In spite of this, sleeping in the south or facing south could help a young student, actor or lawyer.

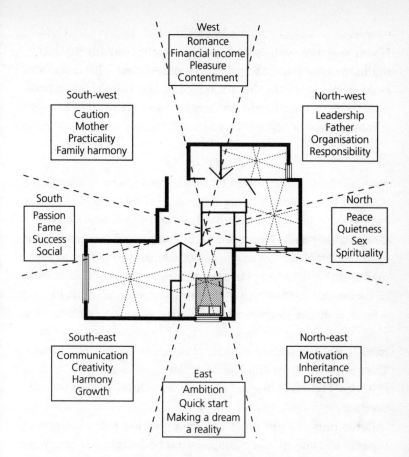

West
Romance
Financial income
Pleasure
Contentment

South-west
Caution
Mother
Practicality
Family harmony

North-west
Leadership
Father
Organisation
Responsibility

South
Passion
Fame
Success
Social

North
Peace
Quietness
Sex
Spirituality

South-east
Communication
Creativity
Harmony
Growth

East
Ambition
Quick start
Making a dream
a reality

North-east
Motivation
Inheritance
Direction

Fig 22 Sleeping east of the centre of your home, or facing east,
can be ideal for building up your career or business

SOUTH-WEST

I do not usually recommend sleeping in the south-west or facing south-west. This Chi energy can influence the occupants in a way that they become more cautious and possibly find their career or business slows down. I would not recommend this position or direction to anyone who is concerned about their health.

WEST

If you seek more pleasure and romance in your life, try sleeping in the west part of a building or facing west. This is not necessarily the best direction for building up your career or business. It may lead to greater contentment with your life, but someone sleeping here could lose motivation.

NORTH-WEST

Sleeping in the north-west or facing north-west is the classic position for leadership. This is the ideal place for parents or for people who have built up their life and have now reached a more stable phase. North-west Chi energy will bring an influence that can lead to greater responsibility, the ability to organize and the ability to plan ahead. People sleeping here should be better able to take care of the family's needs. Parents I know whose children sleep here while they themselves sleep in a place where energy is less mature, for example the east, find it hard to get the respect of their children or to discipline them. They have put their children in a place where they feel in control. See Figure 23 for an example of adults sleeping in the north-west.

Often one will put one's bed in a position that mixes these types of Chi energy. For example, your bed might be in the west part of your home, but facing south-east. You would then combine the characteristics of the Chi energy of the west and south-east to determine their influence on you whilst you sleep.

A couple in their late 30s asked me to give them a Feng Shui consultation. He worked from home and she did some part-time work from home too. One of their complaints was that they rarely had sex and had so far been unable to have children. I looked at their house and made a plan with the eight directions. It became obvious that his office was where the bedroom should be and the bedroom where the office should be. They

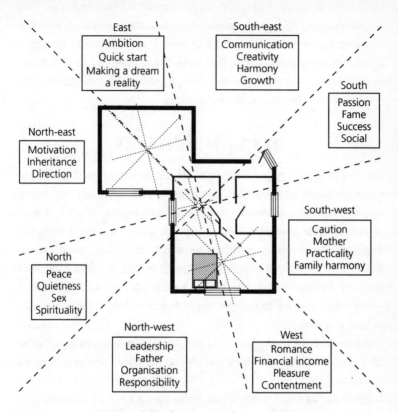

East
Ambition
Quick start
Making a dream
a reality

South-east
Communication
Creativity
Harmony
Growth

South
Passion
Fame
Success
Social

North-east
Motivation
Inheritance
Direction

South-west
Caution
Mother
Practicality
Family harmony

North
Peace
Quietness
Sex
Spirituality

North-west
Leadership
Father
Organisation
Responsibility

West
Romance
Financial income
Pleasure
Contentment

Fig 23 Adults sleeping in the north-west

changed rooms, placed his desk to the east of the centre of the building and turned it so that he also faced east as he worked. They moved their bed into the north part of their house and turned it so that the top of their heads pointed towards east. Within a month she called me to say that their sex life had improved dramatically and that she was now pregnant. He found he could work much better in his new location. Why? Working in the east and facing east placed him within a type of Chi energy that helped him be more active, take ideas, put them into practice and build up his career. By moving their bed to the north part of the house, they became influenced by the Chi energy of the north whilst in bed. Part of this Chi energy's character is related to sex. Turning the bed so the top of their heads point east, they were stimulated by a more active Chi energy, hence the more active sex life.

DESK AND CHAIRS

The art of choosing a place to work or sit involves, first, being clear about what you want to achieve and secondly, deciding which kind of Chi energy will be most helpful to you. If you could choose anywhere in a building to sit you have 512 options. Eight areas within the whole building, eight areas within the room and eight directions in which you can face. Just like my example with the bed you can add the influence of 3 different types of Chi energy to get the blend of Chi energy that is best for you.

Apart from the position and direction, you should try, if possible, to sit so that you face the rest of the room and the door to the room.

Here are examples of places I often recommend to work in.

IN THE EAST FACING EAST

This is ideal if you are starting a new career or business, in the early stages of your working life, or for a young person. The Chi energy of the east helps stimulate a quick start, makes you more active and increases the ability to make your dream a reality. By placing yourself in the east part of a building, the east part of a room, and turning your desk so you face east, you will receive the strongest effect. Choosing south-east will be more subtle. I work from home, and I have tried using various rooms in my home and various places in each room. The place that I get most of the work done is sitting in the east, facing east, even though I have my back to the rest of the room and door. I hung a very large mirror on the wall beside me so that I can see the door and the rest of the room without turning round.

IN THE NORTH-WEST FACING SOUTH-EAST

This is the classic position for the leader or chairman of a company. The Chi energy of the north-west helps to develop organizational skills, along with the ability to plan ahead and generate feelings of responsibility. In addition, the position places the head of a company where he or she is surrounded by Chi energy associated with respect, authority and trust. All are essential qualities for someone in a leadership position.

I have recommended this to chairmen of large companies and they have noticed quite remarkable results in terms of the way their colleagues perceive them. One woman client was having problems with two employees who resented her position. When she changed her office to be in the north-west and face south-east, everyone, except these two employees, preferred the new arrangement. Both the employees she was having difficulties with later left. Now my client can get on with the work of running the company without the unpleasant distractions of internal company politics.

A famous musician employed me to help whilst he was writing his autobiography. He was sitting in the east part of his home facing south. South is good for expression and fame, east for activity, however he could not sit for more than 30 minutes without having to get up. He was also sitting with his back to the rest of the room and the door. He needed to make quicker progress and finish the book as the publisher was getting impatient. He tried sitting in the east, facing west, which was

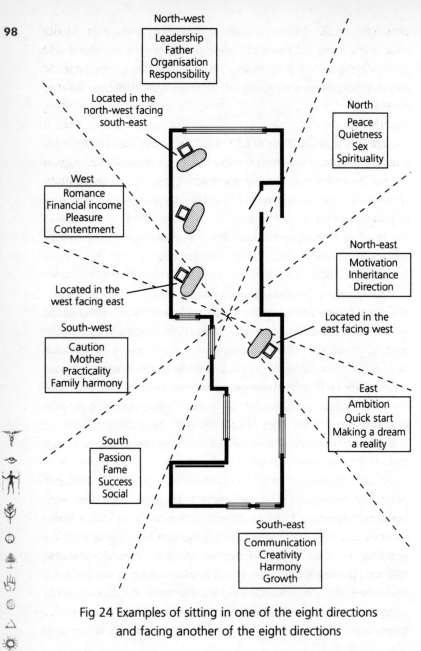

North-west
Leadership
Father
Organisation
Responsibility

Located in the
north-west facing
south-east

North
Peace
Quietness
Sex
Spirituality

West
Romance
Financial income
Pleasure
Contentment

North-east
Motivation
Inheritance
Direction

Located in the
west facing east

Located in the
east facing west

South-west
Caution
Mother
Practicality
Family harmony

East
Ambition
Quick start
Making a dream
a reality

South
Passion
Fame
Success
Social

South-east
Communication
Creativity
Harmony
Growth

Fig 24 Examples of sitting in one of the eight directions
and facing another of the eight directions

PRINCIPLES OF FENG SHUI

practical for the layout of the room and meant he faced the room and door. However, the improvement was small. He noticed the biggest benefit when he sat in the north-west of the room facing south-east. I also advised him on the best time to release the book, in spite of the publisher wanting it three months earlier than the time I suggested. When it came out it stayed in the top ten bestsellers list for more than 14 weeks, reaching the number two position. In his case the Chi energy of the north-west was helpful for responsibility and organization. At the same time, facing south-east helped with communication and creativity.

Using the model of an office, I have given examples of positions and directions to place yourself in Figure 24.

The same principles apply to finding the best location to sit to relax, to eat or for meetings.

For example, sitting in the west part of a home in the evening would be relaxing and help you feel more content. The Chi energy of the west is associated with the evening. Generally, this Chi energy is more settled. Rather like a beautiful red sunset, the Chi energy of the west would be a romantic, satisfying way to end the day. Facing west would intensify the influence of this Chi energy.

Traditionally, at family meals, the father would sit north-west from the centre of the table, facing south-east. This would help establish his position as the head of the household. The mother would sit in the south-west position. Nowadays the north-west position would be helpful for either parent. I would usually recommend this for the primary wage earner. The remaining positions would be suitable for the children, especially the east and north-east for boys, west and south-east for girls.

In meetings, I recommend the chairperson sits in the north-west facing south-east. In a company, other positions can be taken according to the person's role within the company.

Activities that are concerned with public relations, advertising and increasing the company's profile among the public, would be well suited in the south. The south-west would be appropriate for real estate, personnel and matters concerning the welfare of employees. West for tasks relating to financial income, accountancy or the financial director. North for the flow of money or materials within the company. North-east for the company's building or matters concerned with competition. East for investment, expansion and new businesses. South-east for transport and communications.

It is not always possible to find the ideal place for a bed, desk or chairs, therefore part of the skill of a Feng Shui consultant is to create solutions in a limited space. Remember that it is important to make sure the timing of these changes is favourable. It is better to wait than to move into or away from the position of 5 that year, even though you have found a better place. In addition, I would not recommend moving your bed so you begin the new position with the top of your head pointing towards or away from 5. The same applies to your desk.

ALTERING THE FLOW OF CHI ENERGY

Having found the best places to position yourself, the next step is to decide whether to alter the flow of Chi energy through the building. There are many ways of doing this. I will describe those that I have found to be most effective.

The first three are all materials that can be found in the human body–water, salt and iron. Everything has its own flow of Chi energy. It is my belief that, because these materials radiate a type of Chi energy that is in tune with the Chi energy from the same materials when inside the human body, they have a greater ability to influence us. It is almost as though they can communicate to each other better, because they 'speak' the same language.

Seventy per cent of our body is made up of water. For many reasons water has a special significance in our lives. We need to drink water to live. Most of us feel a need to travel to places that have an ocean, sea, river, lake or swimming pool. We evolved from creatures that lived in the sea.

I explained earlier how water Chi energy supports the tree Chi energy of the east and south-east. Therefore, water placed in either of these directions from the centre of a building will build up the Chi energy associated with the occupant's career or business. In the east, water would be more useful for making a quick start, for ambition and putting ideas into practice, whereas in the south-east, water would be better for communication, creativity and developing life harmoniously.

This can be within the east or south-east part of a building or the land. Water features include fountains, ponds, swimming pools, rivers, lakes, an ocean, aquaria, kitchen sink and indoor water fountains.

It is important that the water is fresh and clean. Stagnant or dirty water could have a negative effect.

SEA SALT

Sea salt is considered one of the most yang ingredients in our diet. Taken to excess it has a drying effect that creates extreme cravings for liquids. In Feng Shui, sea salt is used to contract Chi energy and make it more solid.

I sometimes recommend people put it in a small bowl and then place it in the appropriate location. Two to three tablespoons are sufficient and it needs to be changed every one to two months. Some Feng Shui practitioners recommend taking a handful of sea salt and scattering it on the floor where appropriate. Leave it for twenty four hours before cleaning it up.

I often recommend placing a bowl of sea salt next to a door, if the door is to the north-east of the centre of a building. The yang, metal Chi energy of the sea salt has the effect of stabilizing the quickly changing soil Chi energy of the north-east.

The effect of putting a small bowl of sea salt next to a door if situated in the north-east is to help make the occupant's life more stable and less vulnerable to outside influences. The sea salt here can create a more secure environment. If I recommend someone places sea salt in the north-east of a building, I also advise them to put a bowl of sea salt in the south-west. This helps stabilize the movement of energy between the north-east and south-west.

Even if there are no doors in the north-east you can still stabilize the flow of Chi energy by placing small bowls of sea salt in the north-east and south-west.

IRON

This includes items made of cast iron, such as pots, wrought iron, such as a gate, or metals that contain iron. Iron is associated with metal Chi energy, and has the effect of stabilizing the flow of Chi energy. Iron has the effect of altering the flow of the local magnetic field. For this reason large steel beams, iron beds or steel furniture need to be used with care. Although iron has similar properties to sea salt, in my opinion it is not as effective at stabilizing the movement of Chi energy.

A black cast-iron pot could be very effective in the south-west part of a building if you wish to make the Chi energy there more calm and solid. This would also be effective if there is water in the south-west. The iron, metal Chi energy, would help bridge the gap between soil and water Chi energy. For example, if a building has a pond to the south-west, which is not harmonious in the five elements, placing a metal statue between the pond and the building will help create a more harmonious flow of Chi energy. Another example of this would be a large clock

situated in the west or north where you wish to concentrate
103
and contain metal Chi energy.

PLANTS

Plants hold a unique position in a building as they are living
entities and have a more radiant flow of Chi energy. In general,
growing plenty of plants in a building will create a more fresh,
alive atmosphere. In front of internal corners they help move
the Chi energy and avoid stagnation. In external or protruding
corners, plants calm down swirling Chi energy. In a long corridor they slow down fast-moving Chi energy.

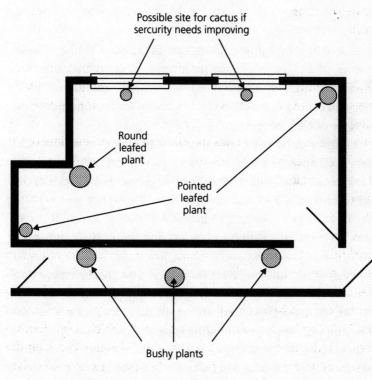

Possible site for cactus if
sercurity needs improving

Round
leafed
plant

Pointed
leafed
plant

Bushy plants

Fig 25 Different plants will create a different effect

PRINCIPLES OF FENG SHUI

Different types of plants will create a different effect. Plants with pointed leaves will tend to help move Chi energy more quickly. These plants are more yang and well-suited to internal corners where the aim is to reduce stagnation. Plants with round floppy leaves are more yin. They tend to calm the flow of Chi energy. Plants with round leaves are effective when placed in front of an external or protruding corner. Bushy plants help slow the flow of fast-moving Chi energy and can work well in long corridors or near doors. Cactus plants are normally considered too prickly for the interior of a building, however some Feng Shui practitioners claim they help deter burglars when placed on a window sill (see Figure 25).

COLOURS

In an existing building colours can be applied through fresh flowers, plants, pictures, picture frames, pieces of art, furniture or other household items. In a new building colours for wall, floor and ceiling decoration can be chosen for their influence on the flow of Chi energy.

Colours can be used to activate, harmonize or subdue Chi energy. Chapters 3 and 5 provide a full description of the Chi energy associated with each of the five elements and each of the eight directions. You will need to decide whether you wish to use the colours of the five elements or those of the eight directions as each uses different colours for the north, north-east, south, south-west and west. These are based on the Nine Ki energies. With the Nine Ki colours first find their element and then the Nine Ki colour of the supporting element. I will use the colours associated with the eight directions in my examples. The principles are the same for either set of colours.

To make the Chi energy more active, use the supporting colour for the Chi energy in that part of the building. For example, dark green in the south part of a building will activate the

fire Chi energy. Dark green, tree Chi energy of the south-east
supports purple, fire Chi energy of the south.

For a building that has a bathroom in the west I often rec-ommend placing red flowers or a red plant in there. A bath-room in the west is not favourable. Red is the colour associat-ed with the west, the red flowers help maintain the flow of metal Chi energy.

Another example would be to use purple to add passion to a bedroom situated in the south-west of a home. Purple fire Chi energy activates the soil Chi energy of the south-west. Conversely, black could be used to subdue the Chi energy in a southern room. Black soil Chi energy would take away some of the Chi energy from the southern, fire Chi energy room.

MIRRORS

As Chi energy behaves in a similar way to light, mirrors can be used to change the direction of the flow of Chi energy in the same way that a mirror reflects light.

Mirrors staggered on either side of a long corridor will move the Chi energy from side to side, slowing its flow along the cor-ridor (see Figure 26).

Large mirrors can also be used to give the impression that a room extends into a missing area (see Figure 27). Standing in this room, looking at the mirror, will create the illusion that space facing the mirror exists behind the mirror. If several mirrors are joined together, the joins make everything in the reflection seem disjointed. The joins need to be hidden with wide ribbons, strips of wood or plants.

With regard to mirrors, they need to be large enough, and positioned so that the reflection does not cut off the top of any of the occupants' heads.

A special mirror that I occasionally recommend in Feng Shui consultations, is a small, round, convex mirror. This has the

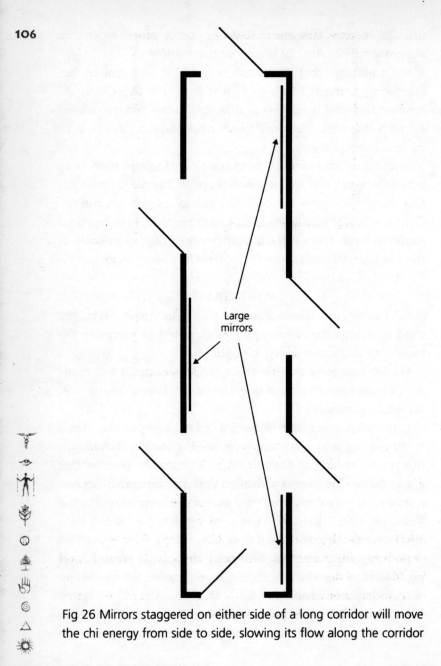

Large
mirrors

Fig 26 Mirrors staggered on either side of a long corridor will move
the chi energy from side to side, slowing its flow along the corridor

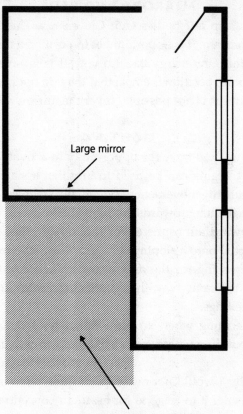

Large mirror

Area that the mirror will create
the impression exists

Fig 27 Large mirrors can also be used to give the impression that a
room extends into a missing area

effect of reflecting and spreading Chi energy. This would be
very useful, for example, when trying to stop Chi energy flowing towards a door.

As well as mirrors, other objects that have a shiny, reflective
surface will have a similar effect.

PRINCIPLES OF FENG SHUI

While we sleep our bodies emit Chi energy. This is part of a cleansing process. It is important not to position a mirror so that it reflects this Chi energy back to you. If you have mirrors in your bedroom, position them so that they do not point towards your bed. If this is not possible, cover the mirrors with a cloth.

LIGHTING

With lighting, you have the opportunity to activate the flow of Chi energy. Lights can be used to brighten a stagnant corner and stimulate the movement of potentially stagnant Chi energy.

Lights that shine upwards are particularly useful for creating a more upward atmosphere. For this reason, they are helpful when directed onto a sloping ceiling, as they help move energy up, compensating for the downward influence of the sloping ceiling. In the same way, these lights are useful in a building with low ceilings.

When deciding where to place lights, try to think of those areas in a building where you wish to keep an active flow of Chi energy.

Personally, I would not recommend fluorescent lighting, as I do not consider it to be good for health or concentration.

CRYSTALS

When light shines onto a multi-faceted round crystal, the effect is to disperse light. Hanging a crystal in a sunlit window will produce a pattern of light on the walls of a room.

This is helpful when you wish to move more Chi energy into a stagnant room. I would recommend hanging crystals in the window of a room that has dark corners or feels dull.

Candles can be used to add fire, warmth and light to a space. I recommend lighting candles in the north-east part of a building or room, when you wish to activate Chi energy there. The north-east has the five element energy of soil and is therefore supported by fire Chi energy. The north-east is a colder direction, so it can benefit from the hot fire. Other directions that would be harmonious are east, south-east and south-west. However, as these areas are already relatively 'hot', it is less likely that fire would be desirable or necessary. Any kind of fire in the south is considered to increase the risk of the building catching fire and is, therefore, not often recommended.

WIND CHIMES

The ringing sound of a wind chime or bell has the effect of vibrating the air, which in turn stimulates the Chi energy. This is considered to have a cleansing effect on the building. When choosing a wind chime it is important to buy one that makes a sound that resonates. Those that are made of metal can be considered to have the properties of the five element metal Chi energy. The wind chime needs to be hung somewhere that it will ring, in order to be effective.

Any sound in a building will influence the movement of Chi energy, so it is therefore worth considering all the various items that make sound and to what extent you can choose versions that make sounds that you find more harmonious. This includes telephones and door bells.

TYPICAL PROBLEM AREAS AND FENG SHUI SOLUTIONS

So far I have described the influence of Chi energy on a building using the principles of yin and yang, the five elements and the eight directions. In this chapter, I will explain how various features of a building or the surrounding landscape influence the flow of Chi energy. At this stage the objective is to understand the way they alter the flow of Chi energy. With experience, you will be able to begin to work out more accurately the effect of each of these features, dependent on which direction they are from the centre of a building.

The following are examples of classic Feng Shui problem areas.

A BUILDING AT THE TOP OF A T-JUNCTION

This is when a building is located at the top of a T-junction (see Figure 28), so that as cars approach the junction, they direct the flow of Chi energy towards your building. This has the effect of placing the occupants of the building in a position where they are in the path of a funnel of fast-moving Chi energy. The busier the road, the more intense this flow of Chi energy will be.

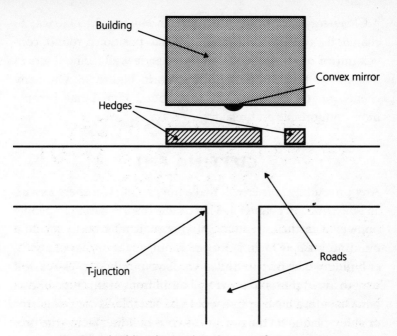

Fig 28 A building located at the top of a T-junction

I remember the first clients I encountered had a house at the top of a T-junction. It was a semi-detached home, close to a busy, main road, with a side road pointing straight at their house. They both felt unsettled in their home. He wanted to go out a lot. Neither of them could really relax at home.

The solutions are to try to slow down and subdue the flow of Chi energy, as well as to deflect some of the Chi energy in another direction. To slow the movement they grew a hedge and bushes in the front garden. Any living vegetation will have its own flow of Chi energy. As the Chi energy directed by the road and traffic passes through the hedge, it has a similar effect as water passing through a sponge. The Chi energy from the road meets a resistance, as it becomes immersed in the Chi energy of the hedge, and as a result begins to move more slowly.

Chi energy also behaves in a similar way to light. One way to change the direction of Chi energy is to position a round, convex mirror or shiny plaque on the outside wall facing the road that points towards the building, as in Figure 28. Once my clients put this into practice they found their home became more comfortable and relaxing.

CUTTING CHI

Any protruding corner will make the passing Chi energy swirl, as I described in chapter 1. This can be disorientating to people immersed in this swirling Chi energy. It may occur inside a building, such as in an L-shaped room, or the corner of another building may be pointing towards your building. The easiest way to avoid this is to grow a plant in front of this type of corner. Outside, a bush or tree would be suitable. A convex mirror or shiny plaque on the outside of your building facing the protruding corner of another building will reflect and spread out some of the cutting Chi (see Figure 29).

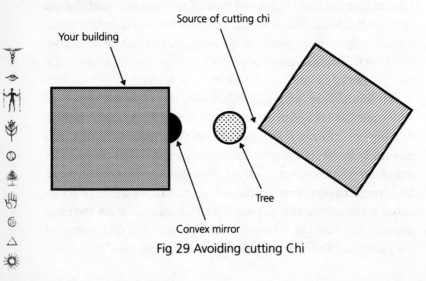

Source of cutting chi

Your building

Tree

Convex mirror

Fig 29 Avoiding cutting Chi

Chi energy tends to speed up and flow quickly along a corridor. To slow the Chi energy you can place indoor plants, staggered on either side of the corridor. Another option would be to hang large mirrors at staggered points on either side of the corridor. (See Figures 25 and 26.) Shiny surfaces will make the movement of Chi energy faster and I would try to avoid this type of floor.

STAIRS

Stairs link the different floors of a building and carry the flow of Chi energy between floors. In addition, the stairs often have a relatively high traffic flow of people. This makes them a busy place in terms of Chi energy.

STAIRS IN THE CENTRE OF A BUILDING

Stairs in the centre of a building are considered to separate the family. To try to calm this busy flow of Chi energy in the centre of a building use sea salt, iron or stone. The particular compass direction from the centre of the home will help you decide which would be more helpful.

STAIRS LEADING TO THE FRONT DOOR

Stairs that lead straight to the front door or any door that opens to the outside, are considered to direct and focus Chi energy moving between the floors straight at the door. This can lead to a deficiency in Chi energy within the building. This situation is often considered to lead to financial difficulties.

A convex mirror can be used to reflect some of the Chi energy away from the door. In addition a large, leafy plant between the stairs and door will help slow the movement of Chi energy towards the door. A wind chime hung between the stairs and door could also help spread the Chi energy out (see Figure 30).

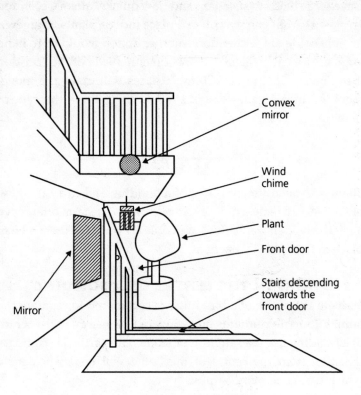

Fig 30 Directing Chi energy away from the front door

FRONT DOOR IN LINE WITH THE BACK DOOR

When you open the front door and you are able to see the back door, Chi energy is free to move quickly between the doors. More Chi energy is likely to enter the building and leave again without circulating through the building.

I recommend growing plants between the doors to slow the movement between them. Mirrors can be used to deflect the Chi energy into other parts of the building. A wind chime will help spread the Chi energy each time it rings (see Figure 31).

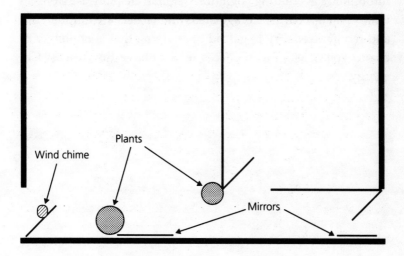

Fig 31 Plants and mirrors slow the movement of Chi energy between the front and back doors

NARROW ROOMS

When you apply the eight directions to a narrow building or narrow room, you will see how some directions take up large areas of the space, whereas other directions have very little space. This makes it less likely that the occupants can benefit from a balance of all eight types of Chi energy.

Large mirrors can be used to create the impression that the room is twice as wide. Remember it is better not to have mirrors facing each other or facing a bed.

CLUTTER

Any kind of clutter in a building will slow the flow of Chi energy and increase the risk of stagnation. To refresh the Chi energy throughout a building, organize regular cleaning sessions in which all cupboards, storage areas and closets are emptied out and reorganized. Try to get rid of anything that is no longer of use to you. Clean, open spaces tend to have the freshest Chi energy.

A CHECKLIST FOR BUYING OR SURVEYING YOUR OWN HOUSE

The following is a simple checklist you can apply to your existing home or workplace, or to a new building you intend moving into. This includes the most important considerations I use when advising someone on moving to a new building. It is not an exhaustive list of all the aspects a Feng Shui consultant should consider.

1 THE DIRECTION OF YOUR MOVE

Check that the direction you and your family are moving in, in a particular year, is in harmony with the Chi energy of your and their Nine Ki Year numbers. See chapter 9.

2 THE WELL-BEING OF THE PREVIOUS OWNERS

Try to find out what happened to the previous owners. If they were happily married, had successful careers and enjoyed good health, it is more likely that the home has favourable Chi energy. A home where the previous owners suffered ill health, divorce or bankruptcy will need attention.

3 EXPOSURE TO SUN

Good exposure to sunlight and natural light brings more Chi energy into a building and helps keep Chi energy moving. A bright, sunlit building is unlikely to suffer from stagnation. See chapters 2 and 3.

4 THE POSITION OF WATER

Find out if there is any type of water close to the building. If there is, check the direction in which the water is located relative to the centre of the building. East or south-east would be ideal. See chapters 4, 5 and 6.

5 THE POSITION OF
THE MAIN GATE AND DOOR

Check the direction, from the centre the building, of the main entrance or gate to the land and the main door to the building. Directions that are generally favourable are east, south-east, west and north-west. Entrances in the north-east and south-west require the most attention. See chapter 8.

6 THE EFFECT OF THE LANDSCAPE

In Feng Shui it is recommended that the high ground is to the north, with the south side of a building open to sunlight.

Check whether any roads point at the building. See chapter 11. Being close to a busy road has a disturbing effect on the flow of Chi energy in a building.

Avoid a building that is located in the shadow of another building. This deprives your building of sunlight and, therefore, reduces Chi energy indoors.

A river that runs away from a building can in effect take Chi energy away from a building, leaving it deficient of Chi energy.

Try to find out whether people are successful in that area and what they are successful for. See chapter 9.

Some Feng Shui schools advise against moving into a building from which you can see another building where people are

One problem traditional Feng Shui practitioners did not have to deal with was electrical radiation and toxic waste. Take the time to locate any high voltage electrical power lines, transformers, electrical substations, electric railway lines and microwave transmitters. Opinions vary on what a safe distance is. I would suggest a home should be at least 800 metres away from any significant electrical radiation. In my opinion, a site within 50 kilometres of a nuclear power plant or waste processing plant, would not be good Feng Shui. A land survey will determine whether the site has been polluted by toxic waste.

Land where the vegetation appears healthy and has a thriving wildlife is generally a good sign for a healthy site.

7 SITING OF TREES

Large trees to the south and east of a building will deprive the building of sunlight and make it more deficient in terms of Chi energy. Trees to the north and north-west are considered advantageous.

8 THE POSITION OF THE KITCHEN

The ideal position for a kitchen is to the east or south-east from the centre of a building. The north-east is considered particularly unhelpful. See chapter 8.

9 THE POSITION OF THE BATHROOM AND TOILET

North, north-west, east or south-east are directions that are potentially less of a problem than north-east, south-west, west or south. Out of all these, a bathroom or toilet in the north-east is considered least desirable. See chapter 8.

Bathrooms and toilets that have their own windows are less of a problem. See chapter 8.

10 OPTIONS FOR THE BEDS, STUDY AND LAYOUT OF THE ROOMS

When looking throughout a building check that you will be able to position your beds, desk and chairs in favourable locations facing a helpful direction. See chapter 10.

11 THE SHAPE OF THE HOUSE

Look at the shape of the building. Rectangular, octagonal or round are the easiest shapes. If the building is an irregular shape, determine which areas are extensions or missing spaces, check their direction from the centre of the building and look up how they affect the flow of Chi energy. See chapters 6 and 7.

Certain schools of Feng Shui will examine the shape of a building to see if it resembles an object from real life. For example, a building whose floorplan outline looks like a knife or cleaver would not be considered desirable.

12 STAIRS

Stairs that lead straight to the front door make a building less desirable in terms of Feng Shui. See chapter 11.

Stairs that cut through the centre of a building can disrupt the flow of Chi energy and are, therefore, considered unfavourable. See chapter 11.

GUIDELINES FOR THE PRACTICE OF FENG SHUI

In my experience there is no such thing as the perfect Feng Shui building. Every building has something that alters and disturbs the flow of Chi energy. The primary question is whether this has a negative influence on the occupants' lives. When you apply Feng Shui to a building, the first objective is to discover whether the occupants are having problems themselves. If they are not, then the areas of their home that would normally be considered unfavourable are obviously not creating difficulties for these people. Try not to create problems that do not exist.

If the occupants are having problems, make sure you can match their problems with your assessment of their building. Once you have achieved this, the potential solutions will become clear.

I sometimes think of myself as a Feng Shui detective, as a considerable amount of my time is taken trying to find the cause of the occupants' problems. Is it the direction and timing of their move? What Nine Ki phase are they in? How does their building affect them? It is only once I have found out why they are having difficulties, that I can feel confident about finding the best Feng Shui recommendations for them.

One example of how this might work is a client whose career in the city of London was going well. However, the relationship she was in had finished over six months ago, and she was keen to start anew. As we were talking I made up a simple Nine Ki astrology chart for her, and for her previous boyfriend. From their charts, they appeared very well matched, and it turned out she still had strong feelings towards him. I checked her home and move to this home. Once I had completed my investigations I went on to find the best place for a water feature, along with a number of other recommendations for her home. Next, I found a good date for her to send him a simple card. The date was chosen so that she would be in an energetic and expressive phase, and he more relaxed. I also found the best direction in which to start her day. She sent the card and later went away on a skiing holiday she had previously arranged. When she returned she started implementing my Feng Shui recommendations. Soon after, the doorbell rang. To her amazement there was her previous boyfriend. He proposed to her on the doorstep.

When you start using Feng Shui I would advise you to keep it very simple. Start by finding the yin and yang sides of the building. Develop the ability to determine what interior design features make a building more yin or yang. Once you have become experienced at using yin and yang, move on to the five elements. Then, when you feel confident with the five elements, start using the eight directions.

In my opinion, people often make the mistake of starting at the top, with the eight directions. Rather like a building with no foundation, it is easy to waver and collapse when confronted with real-life problems. Feng Shui takes time to learn.

The quickest way is to learn one simple aspect of Feng Shui and to then keep applying it to as many buildings as you can. As you do this, check with the occupants to find out if this has the effect you predicted. Then go on to the next aspect you wish to learn.

Above all, keep your common sense! Often, the most effective Feng Shui solutions are very simple and subtle. Change the things in a building that are most practical, before attempting anything that requires major changes.

Remember my definition of Feng Shui: the art of building design that is solely focused on the success of the occupants. It is the occupants who count. In my experience, it is only by following the lives of the occupants that I can really find out how my recommendations affect their lives. I would highly recommend that any student of Feng Shui does the same.

A FENG SHUI
CONSULTATION

There is no standard Feng Shui consultation and each practitioner will have their own style. These can vary from a visit to a building and verbal advice, to a visit with a comprehensive written report. Some practitioners will carry out rituals to change the flow of Chi energy while they are there. It is also possible to have a Feng Shui consultation by post.

For my own Feng Shui consultations, I visit the building and meet the occupants. During the time I am there I find out their dates of birth, when they moved to the building and where from. This enables me to make up their Nine Ki chart and calculate the direction they moved to this building.

Next, I listen to how their lives changed since they moved to this building and find out what they want to achieve from their Feng Shui consultation. Once I have carefully collected all the information I need, I then look at the building.

If they do not have floorplans, I measure the building and make my own plans. At the same time I will take compass readings and when I am satisfied that I have got a consistent reading, I mark this on the plans.

While I am in the building I like to discuss the various options in terms of Feng Shui solutions so that I can get an idea of what changes they are prepared to make. If appropriate I will also walk around their property and note any important features. I also pay attention to the neighbourhood, surrounding buildings and local landscape.

Once I am back in my office, I draw out the plans and lay the grid of the eight directions over each floor of their building. In addition I will check on a map to see if there is any water close to the building.

I personally have a systematic approach to writing my Feng Shui reports which methodically takes me through every aspect I use for Feng Shui. When all this, including their Nine Ki phase and the influence of their move is complete, I can then work on solutions. For certain solutions I will calculate a choice of the best dates to implement them.

Once all of the written report and drawings are complete, I send the information to my clients. We can then talk on the telephone if they need further explanation, or help in implementing my recommendations.

For Feng Shui consultations by post I ask people to write down all the information I need and send it with drawings, a local map and photographs.

FINDING A
FENG SHUI CONSULTANT

At the time of writing this book, Feng Shui is still relatively new outside the orient. However, there are already embryonic Feng Shui societies and associations springing up. At this time there are no recognized qualifications or training courses. This means that it is up to you to ask the right questions if you wish to ensure you have the Feng Shui practitioner that best suits your needs. Experience can vary from a few weekend courses to more than 40 years experience. There are also many different styles of Feng Shui.

The following is a list of questions I have prepared to help you find the best practitioner for your requirements.

1   Find out how they have learnt Feng Shui. Due to the lack of Feng Shui courses, many practitioners will have previously studied some form of oriental medicine such as acupuncture, shiatsu or Chinese herbal medicine. They will often be qualified in one of these professions and be a member of their appropriate professional association. Other practitioners may have a background in oriental arts like Tai Chi or Qi Kong. It is more common now for people with an interior design background to become involved in Feng Shui. If you are seeking a professional approach to

Feng Shui the above will help find a Feng Shui practitioner with professional qualifications in a related field. You
could also find out how long they have been working as a
Feng Shui practitioner and what type of clients they have
worked with.

2   If you have a preference for a certain style of Feng Shui ask
what type of Feng Shui they practise. See Introduction.

3   Find out what is included in the consultation. Some practitioners will include Nine Ki astrology, others do not.
Some will provide dates for implementing their recommendations. Some practitioners will carry out rituals to
change the flow of energy during your consultation.

4   Ask about fees. A practitioner may be able to give you a
fixed fee for the whole consultation, others will charge by
the hour. It is important to be clear on what this includes.
Does the fee cover a written report, travel time, travelling
expenses and ongoing advice after the consultation?

5   Find out how long the practitioner intends to spend with
you. Typical consultations range from one to two hours.

6   If you feel unsure, ask if you can contact his or her clients
for references.

You will tend to get the most out of a Feng Shui consultation if
you feel the practitioner is someone you can trust, communicate with and who is good at his or her job. If you are making
an appointment by telephone, talk with the practitioner in
person so you can get a feeling of how well you can work
together.

PRINCIPLES OF FENG SHUI

ADDITIONAL
INFORMATION

Simon Brown works as a full-time Feng Shui consultant, lecturing on Feng Shui in both Great Britain and the USA.

To find out more about a Feng Shui consultation with Simon Brown call 0171 431 9897 or write to:

Simon Brown
PO Box 10453
London
NW3 4WD

Simon Brown can also be contacted on e-mail. Number 106025.3515@compuserve.com.

RECOMMENDED READING

I have included my own opinions for each book.

Feng Shui Made Easy by William Spear, HarperCollins*Publishers*.
ISBN: 0 06 251023 1.
   An easy to read introduction to the Form School of Feng Shui, with practical help in identifying your own objectives with Feng Shui.

The Feng Shui Handbook by Derek Walters, Aquarian Press.
ISBN: 0 85030 959 X.
   An in-depth study of the five elements in Feng Shui along with the Eight House school of Feng Shui.

Nine Star Ki by Michio Kushi, One Peaceful World Press.
ISBN: 0 9628528 0 5.
   A highly informative introduction to Nine Ki, with well-written chapters explaining how Nine Ki works. Provides information on relationships and moving.

Feng Shui and Destiny by Raymond Lo, Tynron Press.
ISBN: 1 85646 026 6.

An interesting book describing what can be achieved with the Flying Star school of Feng Shui.

The Feng Shui Handbook, Master Lam Kam Chuen, Gaia Books.
ISBN: 1 85675 047 7.

A beautifully illustrated introduction to the Compass school of Feng Shui.

FUTURE BOOKS BY SIMON BROWN

FILL YOUR HOME WITH
HEALTH, WEALTH AND HAPPINESS

A comprehensive, highly illustrated guide to the Compass style of Feng Shui. The information is easy to use with pictures taking you through every step of applying Feng Shui to your home.

Of further interest. . .

FENG SHUI MADE EASY

DESIGNING YOUR LIFE WITH THE ANCIENT ART OF PLACEMENT

WILLIAM SPEAR

To get the most from life, you need to understand and organize your own personal system within which everything else must function: your environment. This book will show you how. *Feng Shui Made Easy* is a brilliant ride through space, exploring the spirals of life, from the solar system to the double helix of our DNA, landing right at your front door.

Home is where the heart is and the place you call home beats with a vital force you can change – with extraordinary results – using the ancient art of Feng Shui. Learning the secret of how to maximize your energy and health, greatly improve your relationships or create and maintain wealth starts with using this book in your own environment – your home or workplace – to harmonize and bring into balance the original pattern of life.

Here is the unspoken backbone of ancient culture and religion, a profound, detailed and beautifully organized system already used by top performers in every walk of life – from billionaire industrialists to world-class architects and designers – with powerful results.

PRINCIPLES OF NLP

JOSEPH O'CONNOR AND IAN MCDERMOTT

Neuro-Linguistic Programming (NLP) is the psychology of excellence. It is based on the practical skills that are used by all good communicators to obtain excellent results. These skills are invaluable for personal and professional development. This introductory guide explains:

- what NLP is
- how to use it in your life personally, spiritually and professionally
- how to understand body language
- how to achieve excellence in everything that you do

Joseph O'Connor is a trainer, consultant and software designer. He is the author of the bestselling *Introducing NLP* and several other titles, including *Successful Selling with NLP* and *Training with NLP*.

Ian McDermott is a certified trainer with the Society of Neuro-Linguistic Programming. He is the Director of Training for International Teaching Seminars, the leading NLP training organization in the UK.

PRINCIPLES OF
THE ENNEAGRAM

KAREN WEBB

There is a growing fascination with the Enneagram – the ancient uncannily accurate model of personality types linking personality to spirit. Most people can recognize themselves as one of the nine archetypes. This introduction to the subject explains:

- the characteristics of the nine types

- how the system works

- ways of understanding your own personality

- how to discover your true potential and attain it

- ways to enhance your relationships

Karen Webb is an experienced Enneagram teacher, counsellor and workshop leader. She has introduced many people to the system and guided them in using the information to change their lives. She has been employed by many large companies as a management consultant.

PRINCIPLES OF
HYPNOTHERAPY

VERA PEIFFER

Interest in hypnotherapy has grown rapidly over the last few years. Many people are realizing that it is an effective way to solve problems such as mental and emotional trauma, anxiety, depression, phobias and confidence problems, and eliminate unwanted habits such as smoking. This introductory guide explains:

- what hypnotherapy is
- how it works
- what its origins are
- what to expect when you go for treatment
- how to find a reputable hypnotherapist

Vera Peiffer is a leading authority on hypnotherapy. She is a psychologist in private practice in West London specializing in analytical hypnotherapy and a member of the Corporation of Advanced Hypnotherapy.

PRINCIPLES OF
BUDDHISM

KULANANDA

More and more people are turning towards Buddhism, disillusioned by the materialism of our times and attracted by the beauty and simplicity of this way of life. This introductory guide describes the growth of modern Buddhism and explains:

- who the Buddha was

- the ideas and beliefs at the heart of Buddhism

- how to meditate

- the main types of Buddhism in the world today

Kulananda has worked within the Friends of the Western Buddhist Order since 1975. Ordained in 1977, he is now a leading member of the Western Buddhist Order and, as a teacher, writer, speaker and organizer, is devoted to creating contexts in which Westerners can practise Buddhism.

PRINCIPLES OF
SELF-HEALING

DAVID LAWSON

In these high pressure times we are in need of ways of relaxing and gaining a sense of happiness and peace. There are many skills and techniques that we can master to bring healing and well-being to our minds and bodies.

This introductory guide includes:

- visualizations to encourage our natural healing process

- affirmations to guide and inspire

- ways of developing the latent power of the mind

- techniques for gaining a deeper understanding of yourself and others

David Lawson is a teacher, healer and writer. He has worked extensively with Louise Hay, author of *You Can Heal Your Life*, and runs workshops throughout the world. He is the author of several books on the subject, including *I See Myself in Perfect Health*, also published by Thorsons.

FENG SHUI MADE EASY	1 8553 8377 2	£12.99
PRINCIPLES OF NLP	0 7225 3195 8	£5.99
PRINCIPLES OF THE ENNEAGRAM	0 7225 3191 5	£5.99
PRINCIPLES OF HYPNOTHERAPY	0 7225 3242 3	£5.99
PRINCIPLES OF BUDDHISM	1 85538 508 2	£5.99
PRINCIPLES OF SELF-HEALING	1 85538 486 8	£5.99

All these books are available from your local bookseller or can be ordered direct from the publishers.

To order direct just tick the titles you want and fill in the form below:

Name: _____

Address: _____

_____

Postcode: _____

Send to Thorsons Mail Order, Dept 3, HarperCollinsPublishers, Westerhill Road, Bishopbriggs, Glasgow G64 2QT.

Please enclose a cheque or postal order or your authority to debit your Visa/Access account —

Credit card no: _____

Expiry date: _____

Signature: _____

— up to the value of the cover price plus:
UK & BFPO: Add £1.00 for the first book and 25p for each additional book ordered.

Overseas orders including Eire: Please add £2.95 service charge. Books will be sent by surface mail but quotes for airmail dispatches will be given on request.

24–HOUR TELEPHONE ORDERING SERVICE FOR ACCESS/VISA CARD-HOLDERS — TEL: 0141 772 2281.